NEW DIRECTIONS FOR ADULT AND CONTINUING EDUCATION

Ralph G. Brockett, *University of Tennessee, Knoxville*
Susan Imel, *Ohio State University*
EDITORS-IN-CHIEF

Alan B. Knox, *University of Wisconsin, Madison*
CONSULTING EDITOR

# Learning in Groups: Exploring Fundamental Principles, New Uses, and Emerging Opportunities

Susan Imel
*Ohio State University*

EDITOR

Number 71, Fall 1996

JOSSEY-BASS PUBLISHERS
San Francisco

LEARNING IN GROUPS: EXPLORING FUNDAMENTAL PRINCIPLES,
NEW USES, AND EMERGING OPPORTUNITIES
*Susan Imel* (ed.)
New Directions for Adult and Continuing Education, no. 71
*Ralph G. Brockett, Susan Imel,* Editors-in-Chief
*Alan B. Knox,* Consulting Editor

© 1996 by Jossey-Bass Inc., Publishers. All rights reserved.

No part of this issue may be reproduced in any form—except for a brief quotation (not to exceed 500 words) in a review or professional work—without permission in writing from the publishers.

Microfilm copies of issues and articles are available in 16mm and 35mm, as well as microfiche in 105mm, through University Microfilms Inc., 300 North Zeeb Road, Ann Arbor, Michigan 48106-1346.

ISSN 0195-2242    ISBN 0-7879-9891-5

NEW DIRECTIONS FOR ADULT AND CONTINUING EDUCATION is part of The Jossey-Bass Higher and Adult Education Series and is published quarterly by Jossey-Bass Inc., Publishers, 350 Sansome Street, San Francisco, California 94104-1342. Periodicals postage paid at San Francisco, California, and at additional mailing offices. POSTMASTER: Send address changes to New Directions for Adult and Continuing Education, Jossey-Bass Inc., Publishers, 350 Sansome Street, San Francisco, California 94104-1342.

SUBSCRIPTIONS cost $52.00 for individuals and $79.00 for institutions, agencies, and libraries.

EDITORIAL CORRESPONDENCE should be sent to the Editor-in-Chief, Susan Imel, ERIC/ACVE, 1900 Kenny Road, Columbus, Ohio 43210-1090. E-mail: imel.1@osu.edu.

Cover photograph by Wernher Krutein/PHOTOVAULT © 1990.

TCF  Manufactured in the United States of America on Lyons Falls Pathfinder Tradebook. This paper is acid-free and 100 percent totally chlorine-free.

# Contents

EDITOR'S NOTES  1
*Susan Imel*

1. **Group Learning in Adult Education: Its Historical Roots**  3
   *Amy D. Rose*
   The long history of learning in groups in American adult education is traced in this chapter, which concludes with a discussion of how groups have reemerged as an emphasis of current programming.

2. **The Relationship Between Theories About Groups and Adult Learning Groups**  15
   *Susan Imel, Elizabeth J. Tisdell*
   Some theories about groups and group behavior are introduced, and their contribution to the development of adult learning groups is explored.

3. **Types of Group Learning**  25
   *Patricia Cranton*
   Three types of group learning—cooperative, collaborative, and transformative—are illustrated, and a role for the adult educator is suggested for each type.

4. **Group Learning: The Role of Environment**  33
   *Joseph L. Armstrong, Sharon L. Yarbrough*
   Based on their experiences as group facilitators, the authors propose three principles of the group learning process that are related to the environment.

5. **Constructing Group Learning**  41
   *Joe E. Heimlich*
   Strategies for developing group learning activities for adults are discussed, and hints for using groups effectively are provided.

6. **Group Learning in the Workplace**  51
   *G. Wayne West*
   Changes in the workplace that encourage learning in groups are reviewed, and the role of dialogue in group learning is described.

7. Group Learning and Technology 61
*Brad Cahoon*
The role of groups in understanding and using technology is illustrated with examples from the workplace and Internet-based instruction.

8. Transforming Groups: 71
Developing Practitioner Inquiry Communities
*Cassandra Drennon, Diane L. Foucar-Szocki*
Examples of two practitioner inquiry networks are used to portray how learning in groups can contribute to staff development and program improvement in adult literacy education.

9. Book Groups: Communities of Learners 81
*Sandra Kerka*
The informal learning that takes place in book discussion groups helps adults acquire self-knowledge and construct new meanings by connecting text and life.

10. Summing Up: 91
Themes and Issues Related to Learning in Groups
*Susan Imel*
Themes emerging from the previous chapters are delineated and questions raised about adult learning groups. Future directions for further exploration of group learning in adult education are suggested.

INDEX 97

# Editor's Notes

A great deal of adult learning occurs in groups. Some of this learning takes place in formal settings under the facilitation of an instructor, but much of it happens in informal settings through discussion structured by adult learners. If asked, most adult educators would say that learning in groups is a fundamental tenet of adult education, and in fact, group theory once played a major role in shaping the field. However, the topic of learning in groups has been relatively unexamined in the field's recent literature.

As adult educators, many of us assume that group learning is inherently good and use groups extensively in practice. We may not, however, have given much thought to how and why we use groups. Knights (1993) observes that "the pressures of day-to-day life in institutions are such that time and inclination to think about the puzzling and often bizarre aspects of group . . . life is lacking" (p. 185). The purpose of this sourcebook is to examine selected facets of the current status of learning in groups in adult and continuing education. By exploring some associated theoretical concepts and describing some specific contexts in which adults learn in groups, the chapters in the sourcebook will provide opportunities for adult educators to reflect on their use of groups as well as the status of group learning in the field.

In the opening chapter, Amy D. Rose sets the stage for the remainder of the sourcebook by interpreting the historical roots of group learning in American adult education, highlighting the contributions of leaders such as Lindeman, Follett, Studebaker, and Lewin. She examines how ideas about group learning have changed, the implications of these changes, and how the tensions between individualization and group process have affected the development of a coherent theory of adult education.

The next four chapters focus on some theories and concepts related to learning in groups. In Chapter Two, Elizabeth J. Tisdell and I review some of the literature about groups and group behavior. We draw on our experiences using adult learning groups to relate theory to practice in three areas: attending to group process, forming groups, and addressing power and conflict.

Types of group learning is the topic of Chapter Three. Using Habermas's three domains of human interests and knowledge as a foundation, Patricia Cranton distinguishes between cooperative, collaborative, and transformative group learning and describes for each type its special characteristics, the nature of the learning goals, and the roles of the educator.

The role of the environment in group learning is examined in depth in Chapter Four. Based on their experiences as group facilitators, Joseph L. Armstrong and Sharon L. Yarbrough propose three principles they believe are central to the group learning process and describe how a group's social and institutional contexts affect its internal and external environment and, hence, its learning.

In Chapter Five, Joe E. Heimlich provides practical advice about using the unique characteristics of the group to construct learning activities. In addition to reviewing some methods for group learning, he also lists tips for facilitators.

How group learning plays out in practice is the theme of Chapters Six, Seven, Eight, and Nine, with each focusing on a particular milieu. In Chapter Six, G. Wayne West explores group learning in the workplace. Rather than focusing on a specific company, however, he describes how changes in the workplace are creating environments primed for group learning, and he draws connections to adult learning theory.

Although technology is frequently associated with individualizing instruction, in Chapter Seven Brad Cahoon relates it to learning in groups. Using studies of computer skill learning in the workplace and creative examples of technology-based education delivered via the Internet and World Wide Web, he suggests alternative roles for technology in group educational activities.

How learning in groups can transform professional practice is the topic of Chapter Eight. Cassandra Drennon and Diane L. Foucar-Szocki use their experiences working with literacy practitioner inquiry groups to describe two different examples of group learning. One supports the efforts of individuals, whereas the other has transformed the group itself.

In Chapter Nine, Sandra Kerka explores the nature of informal adult learning as it occurs in book groups, discussing as one of her themes "why book groups are not like school." She also points out connections between book groups and adult education.

Themes and issues emerging from the previous chapters are discussed in the summary chapter, with suggestions for future directions given in conclusion.

*Susan Imel*
*Editor*

**Reference**

Knights, B. "Hearing Yourself Teach: Group Processes for Adult Educators." *Studies in the Education of Adults,* 1993, 25 (2), 184–198.

*SUSAN IMEL is senior research specialist at the Center on Education and Training for Employment, College of Education, The Ohio State University, and director of the ERIC Clearinghouse on Adult, Career, and Vocational Education.*

*Education in groups has a long history in American adult education. Modern adult education has reinvigorated the original emphasis on social change through groups.*

# Group Learning in Adult Education: Its Historical Roots

*Amy D. Rose*

Adult educators have come to adopt two somewhat inconsistent views of learning. The first is that learning should be individualized—that people learn best when materials are adapted to meet their particular needs. Hence, since the late 1960s, interest in programmed learning and other approaches to individualization has emerged. The other view, however, posits that adults learn best in groups through the use of discussion and other group methods. Whereas not necessarily antithetical, these two approaches illustrate the wide berth given to perceptions of good practice within adult education. In this chapter, I will focus on some of the issues relating to the rise of the group as one of the principal entities within the educational process. The questions to be examined include: How have our ideas about group learning changed, particularly during the course of the twentieth century? What implications have these changes had on adult education? How have the tensions between individualization and group process affected the development of a coherent theory of adult education?

## Autodidaxy and Club Learning

As Joseph Kett (1994) has pointed out, American mythology, particularly through the nineteenth century, placed great value on the autodidact. Literature was replete with examples of individuals (mostly men) who had pulled themselves up without any formal education. Instead, they had studied assiduously on their own and had, in their own idiosyncratic way, mastered the learning of more educated men. With the aid of published self-help guides, anyone could become educated.

Although individual and solitary learning was considered to be the most effective, reading groups and other self-help associations were viewed as vehicles for enhancing this learning. While people have long come together for the dissemination of information, the nineteenth century saw a change in the idealization of the self-educated person, which in turn gave particular importance to the group as both the arbiter of what was to be learned and the instiller of a formalized discipline. For women especially, groups also provided a much needed support system.

In the nineteenth century, men's and women's groups often served distinctly different needs. Men often joined together to discuss issues of the day and to engage in further study. Such groups are today seen as the precursors of modern professional societies. In the period before the Civil War, learned and scientific societies allowed for the dissemination of new knowledge to both the well-educated public and the few professionals practicing scientific careers during this period. The nature of the group within this conceptualization was purely for diffusion. A secondary function was socializing or, as we would say today, networking (Oleson and Brown, 1976; Oleson and Voss, 1979).

Women were mostly excluded from these societies. They banded together in their own ladies' auxiliaries and in religious groups. Certainly, portions of their work were educative—for example, there was popular education about the evils of alcohol—but the main purpose was the transformation that could be brought about within the individual who had the appropriate information.

Women of the late nineteenth century had fewer options in pursuing education, and the period saw an explosion in women's clubs that were founded to promote disciplined learning among women. Although clubs for women were certainly not new, the sudden proliferation of clubs devoted to literary study was noteworthy. Theodora Penny Martin (1987) put forward several reasons for the growth of clubs at this time. By the late nineteenth century, women in cities had new leisure. The roles of women were changing, and even work outside the home was possible, albeit rare. At the same time, middle-class women had lost their economic importance within the family unit, as their traditional spheres of homemaking had become less entwined with the family's financial status. Since most women accepted the then predominant ideology of the culture of true womanhood, which had made women the repositories of morality, they saw their role within the family as the purveyor of tradition, the holder of culture. Women's clubs allowed these women to reach out to other women within the confines of true womanhood (Martin, 1987).

Men still pursued culture individually, but women sought it through the group. Although, admittedly, women could have read the same guides as men, many felt that they needed more discipline and more help in systematic thinking. Women's education, unlike men's, was not seen as useful but was truly education for its own sake. The women's clubs adhered to an ideal of self-study, providing the systematic study unavailable to most women. By the early twentieth century, when women had more opportunities for higher education, women's clubs shifted their focus to service.

These clubs can be viewed as one means by which women with families could do something for themselves. They allowed escape from the nurturing ideal of the true woman, providing opportunities to leave home and talk to others, all in an essentially nonthreatening atmosphere.

## Expanding Ideas About Groups and Discussion

In the 1920s, new interest was directed toward the education of adults. This was manifested in several ways. The National Education Association (NEA) initiated a Department of Adult Education to deal with the needs of teachers of immigrants. The Carnegie Corporation began a study of the various facets of adult education, culminating in the founding of the American Association for Adult Education (AAAE) in 1926. Adult education caught the public eye. In 1928, *The New Republic* ran a special issue on the subject. Additionally, many new formats continued the nineteenth-century emphasis on self-education. These included the Book-of-the-Month Club, the Town Meeting of the Air, and other approaches to self-culture. As Joan Shelley Rubin (1992) found in her analysis of some of these ventures during the period between the First and Second World Wars, those who were involved with the ventures were committed to an elevation of public consciousness and discourse. But they also continued an earlier propensity to seek an expert to inform the public about what it should read. All of these endeavors stressed the effort of the individual to achieve culture and gentility.

At the same time, philosophers and psychologists were reassessing the process of learning itself. Inspired by Deweyan progressive education, educators of adults became more cognizant of the environment of learning and of the structuring of the learning experience to more closely relate to the adult's actual experienced life. Hence for some educators, although by no means all, the process of education became as important, if not more important, than the content.

Eduard Lindeman is often portrayed as the most important proponent of this new approach within adult education. Best known for his concern that adult education involve social action, Lindeman's view of adult education as a process was his true major innovation. Lindeman popularized the idea of discussion and of the group as central tenets of the educational process and changed the way adult educators viewed the results of their efforts. Lindeman and others working with groups came to their interest through a concern for leadership within communities. Mary Parker Follett, a political writer concerned with social experience as the basis for state structure, was one of Lindeman's contemporaries and a close associate during the 1920s. For Follett, groups formed the basis of the modern experience, meeting multiple needs within the modern state. The group was an extension of the individual, and both had diverse needs and characteristics. If groups were the key to democratic participation, then citizenship training and leadership were essential. Follett saw the work of groups as a skill to be learned through adult education (Follett, 1918; Konopka, 1958).

Follett's thinking about groups paralleled much of Lindeman's work. Like Follett, Lindeman saw group methods as imperative for democracy. Starting with his interest in the community, Lindeman presented the discussion method as a means of conflict resolution within communities and community organizations. Leadership and knowledge about how to handle emotion and bring scientific method into the community decision-making process were at the heart of community action. For Lindeman, conflict was important to any aspect of community action. He stated that "conflict is the only possible method by which ideas can be clarified in group action" (Lindeman, 1921, p. 134).

Leaders' skill lay in bringing conflicting viewpoints out into the open and then helping to mediate the differing solutions, investigating all aspects, and ultimately helping the group to reach a compromise. Discussion leaders needed training—and not just training in listening. They needed to guide the group without imposing their own agenda. Discussion by itself could not solve problems, but it could indicate the appropriate avenues to take when seeking solutions.

According to Lindeman, discussion was "democracy's basic method, the mechanism through which it operates" (Gessner, 1956, p. 90). He envisioned group work as a "tool for free discussion, for helping citizens to establish more effective committee work, and for helping the growth of indigenous leadership" (Konopka, 1958, p. 129).

Since Lindeman's interest in groups coincided with his writing about adult education, he positioned the group as the center of the adult education experience. In fact, adult education was the link between the individual's experience and group action. Lindeman also believed that eventually all adult education groups "sooner or later become social action groups" (Stewart, 1987, p. 52).

Within adult education, groups did not just get together; their purpose was to explain experience and illuminate a situation. Such a task could be accomplished through discussion or organized talk, not through lecture or any other passive transfer of information. Drawing on his use of groups within a psychotherapeutic situation, Lindeman felt that discussion groups allowed individuals "to relate their knowledge . . . to their emotions" (Stewart, 1987, p. 160).

Lindeman's impact on adult education cannot be overestimated. His use of discussion and facilitation within adult education has been widely adopted. While Lindeman provided the social philosophy for groups, his views were strengthened by the growth of interest in groups and group behavior during the 1940s and 1950s.

Another advocate of discussion, albeit with a different focus, was John Studebaker. As superintendent of schools in Des Moines, Iowa, in 1933, Studebaker initiated an experimental forum program. The forums were an attempt to provide what Studebaker called "civic literacy" by bringing forums on public issues to all of the people of Des Moines. Strictly speaking, the forum was a form of public discussion (Studebaker, 1935). In 1934, when Studebaker became U.S. Commissioner of Education, he brought his commitment to forums with him. During his tenure, tremendous growth occurred in the number of forums supported by public funds. The Works Progress Administration (WPA) established a Forum Division that sent out speakers to lead forum discussions. According to Studebaker, the purpose of the forum was to bring about democratic discussion of issues important to an educated citizenry (Ely, 1937).

These forums, based on the ideal of both the New England town meeting and the lyceum, were supposed to provide the information necessary for informed decision making. But the process was very strictly managed and did not allow for the true type of discussion advocated by Lindeman and others. Leaders very carefully controlled what was discussed and the process of discussion itself. The ideal of the forum and local community governance has been a strong theme within adult education, combining both a nostalgia for the past and a desire for social change (Stubblefield and Keane, 1994).

## Reorientation of Adult Education to Groups and Group Theory in the 1940s and 1950s

During the 1920s and 1930s, writers both in children's and adult education began to focus on alternative educational processes that would bring experience into the classroom. Discussion groups were one aspect of this. In the 1940s, writers began to look at group processes more closely and to examine exactly how groups operated. This research took into account the situation of the individual and the particular dynamics of each group, then categorized differing approaches to the creative use of groups in the educative process.

According to Malcolm Knowles and Hulda Knowles, closer study of groups began in the 1930s, when what they call "the modern era" of group dynamics emerged (Knowles and Knowles, 1959, p. 20). The characteristics of this era included the founding of research groups such as the Research Center for Group Dynamics at the University of Michigan; the publication of several journals with a group orientation including *The Journal of Social Issues, Human Relations, and Sociometry;* and the growth of training programs. All these efforts contributed to substantial growth in group dynamics during the late 1940s and early 1950s.

One of the most important areas of research on groups was Kurt Lewin's field theory. Borrowing from physics, Lewin postulated that groups had their own psychological fields, much like electromagnetic fields. The psychological field could be considered to consist of the number of variables affecting the behavior of the group. The scientist's job was to develop methods for observing and analyzing the groups (Lewin, 1951).

The results of this and other research provided information on four areas: leadership training, the invention of new techniques, the study of the culture of groups and large meetings, and community relations and social change

(Knowles and Knowles, 1959). All of these areas were particularly important for the field of adult education, which was just beginning to study the educational process in depth. For adult educators, the understanding of group processes became a central part of the adult education process (Bergevin and Morris, 1950).

In the 1950s, discussion continued to be one of the methods most favored by adult educators. Many books and pamphlets were written for group leaders on how to initiate and manage discussion. In 1948, Cyril Houle laid out what he considered to be the basic principles of adult learning, as conducted within groups. According to Houle, everyone within a group needed to understand the group's goal; there should be a pleasant social atmosphere and a physical environment conducive to learning. Group leaders had to acknowledge their limitations; all members of the group needed to attain some feeling of accomplishment. All individual learning needs had to be met, at least to some extent; group members' own experience and background needed to be incorporated into the course or group experience. The leader had to have some plan, while also making allowances for individual interests. And finally, methods were to be varied; even the most informal groups needed to go beyond discussion to include other formats such as lectures, films, and role play (Houle, 1948).

One of the most important efforts of the period was the use of discussion in projects funded by the Ford Foundation through the Fund for Adult Education (FAE). As John Walker Powell (1960) noted, between 1951 and 1960 the FAE "invested very substantially in a *method* of adult learning; the method of group discussion based on the consecutive study of books and related materials, under non-professional leadership" (p. 1). Powell saw FAE groups as a powerful antidote to the passivity instilled in adults by public education.

Despite the wide acclaim for groups and group learning during the 1950s, there were some who cautioned about over-enthusiasm. When deS. Brunner, Wilder, Kirchner, and Newberry (1959) surveyed adult education research through 1959, they were very skeptical of the complete faith placed by educators on groups and group methods. Research completed up to that time did not confirm the effectiveness of groups in all situations. In fact, some evidence showed that groups hindered intellectual and cognitive development, while aiding the socialization process. Although groups, particularly discussion groups, remained a mainstay of adult education, in the 1960s, the main new thrust of group learning was affective, not cognitive, learning. Through T-groups, consciousness-raising groups, and other self-help organizations, group learning focused on affect rather than on cognitive issues.

## New Uses of Groups: The 1960s and Beyond

Despite the lack of evidence of its efficacy, adult educators have continued to advocate the use of groups, and discussion in particular, as effective means of adult learning. As deS. Brunner, Wilder, Kirchner, and Newberry (1959) had indicated earlier, adult education would continue to take place in groups because the group format was the best allocation of resources. But the 1960s brought to popularity some earlier trends, specifically group methods developed in the areas of intergroup relations, empowerment, and T-groups.

These uses of groups developed out of Lewin's initial work during World War II that established the potential of groups to change behavior, even if they were not as effective in conveying information. Lewin's initial classical study was concerned with consumer habits; specifically, he wanted to determine the most effective method for getting women to change their habits of consumption during wartime rationing. Lewin selected women from all socioeconomic levels and divided them into two groups. One group received a thirty-minute lecture by a nutritionist, followed by a fifteen-minute question-and-answer session. The other group discussed the issue for forty-five minutes in the presence of a nutritionist. A skilled discussion leader led the discussion. The same recipes were given to both groups. The result was that the women from the discussion groups were much more likely to try the new foods than were those from the lecture groups (Lewin, 1942).

Lewin's study has often been cited as an example of the effectiveness of discussion. But as deS. Brunner, Wilder, Kirchner, and Newberry (1959) point out, the series of studies on this issue did not prove this; what the studies did do, however, was show the efficacy of discussion and groups in changing behavior. Because learning and behavior change have often been collapsed as categories in research studies, this distinction has been lost.

**T-Groups.** Lewin's 1940s work on groups and behavior change was further developed in the 1950s by Ron Lippitt, Kenneth Benne, and others. One of the most important innovations was the formulation of the concept of *training-groups* (T-groups). T-groups developed out of a serendipitous event during a teacher training conference on intergroup relations organized by Lewin and his associate in 1946. Continuing Lewin's earlier work, the researchers were studying changes in behavior that occurred after the conference. In order to do this, participant observers, who were sitting in on all sessions, planned meetings during the course of the conference to discuss their observations. At one such meeting, some participants asked to sit in, and consequently they joined the researchers in analyzing events. The analysis of the proceedings soon surfaced as an important and effective learning tool. The participants found the formal program less effective than the feedback from the group (Benne, Bradford, Gibb, and Lippitt, 1974; Miller, 1993).

This finding seemed to be worthy of further study, and a follow-up meeting was planned in 1947, which, in turn, led to the founding of the National Training Laboratories (later the NTL Institute for Applied Behavioral Science) in Bethel, Maine (Benne, Bradford, Gibb, and Lippitt, 1974; Miller, 1993). The National Training Laboratory was designed as a unit within the National Education Association's (NEA) Department of Adult Education to study group processes. Despite the sometimes fractious relationship between the NTL and the NEA, the work of the NTL was highly respected, if not completely viewed as adult education (Luke, 1992).

When Leland Bradford, the executive secretary of the NEA's Department of Adult Education, tried to make T-groups and the laboratory method the cornerstone of adult education, he met resistance from adult educators more concerned with the practical issues of administration and funding. Yet if adult educators resisted a complete marriage with T-groups, they certainly embraced many of the methods—from their adoption of circles to the various approaches such as role play, the emphasis on nonlecture formats, participatory techniques, and an appreciation of the dynamic nature of adult learning (Luke, 1992; Stubblefield and Keane, 1994).

Because T-groups originally grew out of research on intergroup relations, they were initially perceived as an important tool in the emerging area of human relations work. Surprisingly however, the first widespread use of T-groups was as a management tool. T-groups were viewed as a way of helping individuals reassess their relationship with their organizations and reconceptualize their work. By the 1970s, the T-group had fallen out of favor with management groups because of the difficulty of carrying over what was learned into the real world. In the 1960s, when their purpose was perhaps least clear, however, T-groups did enjoy great popularity as a new method for promoting self-analysis and achieving self-actualization. Variants of the T-group included the encounter group, and it is evident today in human relations training (Miller, 1993; Stubblefield and Keane, 1994).

**Education for Empowerment and Social Change.** By the 1980s, many proponents of group learning had returned to Lindeman's original interests—social action and social change. Perhaps in response to the greater potential for individualization, writers—particularly adult educators—began to focus on broader societal needs and the possibility of transformation. Certainly, this emphasis was never fully lost in adult education circles. Myles Horton's Highlander Folk School had maintained social change as a consistent thrust of Highlander and had effectively developed methods for providing an atmosphere to promote change. Additionally, Saul Alinsky developed his own method of community organizing that involved the group's search for problem solving and social change.

Beginning in 1970, the work of Paulo Freire started to have enormous influence in the United States. Freire, a Brazilian educator, believed that individual problem solving as an approach limited the possibility of achieving true social change. He felt that individuals, working together, needed to recast their perceptions of problems and, hence, to find solutions through a new consciousness of the world and their place in it. For Freire, change was not an individual issue, although individual change was an important aspect of how society changed. For Freire, all learning could eventually lead to social change, and his work with illiterate Brazilian peasants illustrated his view that people could be taught to read through the development of text that was both meaningful and problematic. Such a process would also empower these peasants to question the assumptions by which they understood and ordered their world. This questioning could ultimately lead to demands for change. Freire's work has been widely discussed, although its implementation has been scattered. By raising questions about the ways individuals can become empowered within groups, Freire reopened an area of educational inquiry that had not been effectively discussed since Lindeman (Freire, 1970).

A different kind of learning takes place in what can be generically referred to as *self-help groups,* although the term is too weak for the diverse and often potent groups included in the designation. Self-help groups include Alcoholics Anonymous, health-related support groups, and more radical organized groups such as those doing community education and women's groups. On one level, these groups can occupy a nebulous territory between a therapeutic and an educational approach. On another level, they branch out into direct political activities that are not always seen as educational. For example, in the 1970s when they first began, women's consciousness-raising groups overlapped with therapy groups for women. Researchers found that participants in women's consciousness raising tended to have the same kind of change in mind as those in therapy but different views about how that change would occur. Therapy patients tended to think that personal change would be painful, while people in consciousness raising did not (Lieberman and Bond, 1976). Additionally, consciousness raising had a liberatory component at its core (Hart, 1990). Consciousness raising as such has waned, but the idea of mutual support has never been stronger. Different groups are devoted to changing behavior in an almost unlimited fashion, and most recognize the educational component of what they do.

## Conclusion

Groups and group learning have become an element almost inseparable from the basic precepts of adult education. The ideal of innovative methods for groups is almost as sacrosanct as the ideal of individualization. Even within the most traditional courses, those dealing with instruction routinely advise the use of role play, discussion, and other activities designed to encourage a more active, participatory atmosphere. Some of this emphasis seems to be misplaced, given the lack of data to show that such efforts actually lead to cognitive growth. Some confusion exists within the field of adult education, because it simultaneously pursues individualization through distance learning and other such innovative uses of technology, while maintaining the importance of the group for true growth and development.

Although the present interest in groups goes back to Eduard Lindeman, Lewin's subsequent work influenced research. While Lindeman saw discussion as the only true means for rational discourse, Lewin's work indicated where the strength of group learning really lay. Adult educators have always relied on groups, but part of this reliance has come from the divergent goals embedded within the multiple goals of adult education itself. Even in the case of women's clubs, the acquisition of knowledge was only one of several goals. In fact, of greater consequence was the chance to build confidence, self-esteem, and fluency in public speaking—skills that could not be gained in isolation. Today, when the possibility for individualized instruction is greater than ever, the importance of groups has also been iterated. Yet the proponents of group learning still have not grappled with some central questions, such as whether it is an ideological position, a method of learning, or a tool for affective change. While group learning lies at the heart of adult education, the process itself is almost taken for granted. Understanding this shift to taken-for-grantedness can shed light on our current understanding of the meanings and methods of adult education.

## References

Benne, K. D., Bradford, L. P., Gibb, J. R., and Lippitt, R. O. (eds.). *The Laboratory Method of Changing and Learning.* Palo Alto, Calif.: Science and Behavior Books, 1974.

Bergevin, P., and Morris, D. *Group Processes for Adult Education.* Greenwich, Conn.: Seabury Press, 1950.

deS. Brunner, E., Wilder, D. S., Kirchner, C., and Newberry, J. S., Jr. *An Overview of Adult Education Research.* Chicago: Adult Education Association of the U.S.A., 1959.

Ely, M. L. *Why Forums?* New York: American Association for Adult Education, 1937.

Follett, M. P. *The New State, Group Organization, the Solution of Popular Government.* White Plains, N.Y.: Longman, 1918.

Freire, P. *Pedagogy of the Oppressed.* (M. B. Ramos, trans.) New York: Herder & Herder, 1970.

Gessner, R. (ed.). *The Democratic Man, Selected Writings of Eduard C. Lindeman.* Boston: Beacon Press, 1956.

Hart, M. U. "Liberation Through Consciousness Raising." In J. Mezirow and Associates, *Fostering Critical Reflection in Adulthood: A Guide to Transformative and Emancipatory Learning.* San Francisco: Jossey-Bass, 1990.

Houle, C. O. "The Importance of Adult Education." In *Study-Discussion Group Techniques for Parent Education Leaders.* Chicago: National Congress of Parents and Teachers, 1948.

Kett, J. *The Pursuit of Knowledge Under Difficulties.* Stanford, Calif.: Stanford University Press, 1994.

Knowles, M., and Knowles, H. *Introduction to Group Dynamics.* New York: Association Press, 1959.

Konopka, G. *Eduard C. Lindeman and Social Work Philosophy.* Minneapolis: University of Minnesota Press, 1958.

Lewin, K. *The Relative Effectiveness of a Lecture Method and a Method of Group Discussion for Changing Food Habits.* Washington, D.C.: National Research Council, 1942.

Lewin, K. *Field Theory in Social Science: Selected Theoretical Papers.* New York: HarperCollins, 1951.

Lieberman, M. A., and Bond, G. R. "The Problem of Being a Woman: A Survey of 1,700 Women in Consciousness-Raising Groups." *Journal of Applied Behavioral Science,* 1976, 12 (3), 363–380.

Lindeman, E. C. *The Community: An Introduction to the Study of Community Leadership and Organization.* New York: Association Press, 1921.

Luke, R. A. *The NEA and Adult Education: A Historical Review, 1921–1972.* Sarasota, Fla.: R. A. Luke, 1992.

Martin, T. P. *The Sound of Our Own Voices: Women's Study Clubs 1860–1910.* Boston: Beacon Press, 1987.

Miller, N. *Personal Experience, Adult Learning and Social Research: Developing a Sociological Imagination In and Beyond the T-Group.* Adelaide: University of South Australia Centre for Human Resources, 1993.

Oleson, A., and Brown, S. (eds.). *In Pursuit of Knowledge in the Early American Republic: American Scientific and Learned Societies from Colonial Times to the Civil War.* Baltimore: Johns Hopkins University Press, 1976.

Oleson, A., and Voss, J. (eds.). *The Organization of Knowledge in Modern America, 1860–1920.* Baltimore: Johns Hopkins University Press, 1979.

Powell, J. W. *Research in Adult Group Learning in the Liberal Arts.* Fund for Adult Education, 1960.

Rubin, J. S. *The Making of Middlebrow Culture.* Chapel Hill: University of North Carolina Press, 1992.

Stewart, D. *Adult Learning in America: Eduard Lindeman and His Agenda for Lifelong Education.* Malabar, Fla.: Krieger, 1987.

Stubblefield, H. W., and Keane, P. *Adult Education in the American Experience: From the Colonial Period to the Present.* San Francisco: Jossey-Bass, 1994.

Studebaker, J. W. *The American Way: Democracy at Work in the Des Moines Forums.* New York: McGraw-Hill, 1935.

*AMY D. ROSE is associate professor of adult continuing education at Northern Illinois University, DeKalb.*

*The literature is replete with theories about groups and group behavior. The authors describe how some of these theories can contribute to the development of adult learning groups.*

# The Relationship Between Theories About Groups and Adult Learning Groups

*Susan Imel, Elizabeth J. Tisdell*

As discussed in Chapter One, the idea of learning in groups is fundamental to American adult education. Adult educators tend to view learners working in groups in a positive light, believing that the group environment enhances learning. But groups can also detract from learning. According to Knights (1993, p. 185), "groups [can] exert powerful influence both to advance and to obstruct learning. A group can be an environment in which people invent and explore symbolic structures for understanding the world, learning from each other and trying out for themselves the discourse of the domain of knowledge they seek to acquire. Alternatively, groups can encourage conformity, squander time and energy on ritual combat, revel in failure, and generally engage in all sorts of fantasy tasks that have little or nothing to do with learning."

As adult educators, we want to ensure that groups are positive forces that contribute to learning rather than negative experiences that diminish learning and turn participants off to the idea of learning in groups. Although much of what happens in learning groups may be beyond our control, an understanding of groups and group process can contribute to positive group outcomes. In this chapter, we examine some of the theories about groups and group behavior and, based on our own experiences in using groups, suggest ways these theories can contribute to the development of adult learning groups. To set the context, we begin with some comments about the status of the literature base on groups and group behavior, followed by observations on learning groups in adult education.

## Setting the Context

In their review of research related to small groups, Levine and Moreland (1990, p. 586) observe that although "the field is quite vigorous, [it] . . . is badly fragmented as evidenced by the failure of researchers working on related problems to acknowledge one another's work," a situation that they attribute to the field's interdisciplinary nature. After searching for literature to use as the basis for this chapter, we can appreciate Levine and Moreland's assessment. A vast literature on the topic of groups and group behavior does exist, but adult educators have used little of it to support the development of theories about learning groups. Furthermore, most of the adult education literature on learning in groups focuses on group process rather than on learning. Limited efforts (see, for example, Dechant, Marsick, and Kasl, 1993; Kasl, Marsick, and Dechant, 1992) have been made to connect theories about group process with adult learning theories. Issues related to power, including race and gender, are also noticeably absent from the adult education literature on groups.

As we considered how to apply theories about groups and group behavior to adult learning groups, another problem arose. Most theories are about established, on-going groups, and most of the adult education literature assumes the group has a facilitator. In adult education, however, many kinds of learning groups exist, ranging from informal discussion groups lasting decades to informal ad hoc groups with a life span of thirty minutes. Also, some groups may only facilitate individual learning, but at other times, the group, as an entity, may learn. How can theory inform such a wide range of learning groups? Does theory have any application to groups with a limited life span, or can it be applied only to groups that have an opportunity to develop a history? Also, what is the relevance of theory to unfacilitated groups?

Faced with the fragmented literature and the diverse use of learning groups in adult education, we decided on the following course. With a few exceptions, we selected literature that has been developed by adult educators as the basis for the chapter; in some places, we include examples of our own experiences using learning groups to support the literature. Although these experiences emerge from our work as facilitators and professors of graduate-level courses, they are with adult learners, and they do range from ad hoc to project groups extending throughout the life of the course. We indicate when we are discussing the group as a whole or smaller subgroups. We also assume that this information is going to be used by a facilitator or group leader who has some responsibility for directing the learning group.

Much of what happens in groups is interrelated and occurs simultaneously. At the same time that groups are attending to their functions or purposes, for example, they are also evolving and developing. To relate theory to the practice of learning groups, we have selected three connected areas: attending to group process, forming groups, and addressing power and conflict.

## Attending to Group Process

Like most groups, learning groups have goals or purposes that are supposed to be achieved through the collective efforts of the group. Studies of how groups function in order to achieve their goals have resulted in a great many theories about group concepts and process, including theories about boundary, task, role, projection, power, authority, and development (Foley, 1992; Jaques, 1991). Areas of group process that affect learning groups are maintenance and task functions and group development. In addition, the facilitator's role vis-à-vis group process also affects learning outcomes.

**Maintenance and Task Functions.** Group theorists have developed a system that classifies the work of groups into maintenance functions and task functions (Cragan and Wright, 1991; Jaques, 1991). Sometimes referred to as the *social-emotional functions,* group maintenance functions are those that contribute to building and maintaining relationships and cohesiveness among group members and include encouraging, mediating, gatekeeping, following, and relieving tension. Task functions are those that help the group do its work and include initiating, information seeking, information giving, clarifying, elaborating, and summarizing (Jaques, 1991).

In a well-functioning group, the members assume responsibility or roles for carrying out the group's task and maintenance functions. Decisions about who will perform group functions may be conscious or unconscious, may or may not be connected to a group leadership role, and may or may not be directed by a facilitator. Group members are much more likely to be proactive about assuming responsibility for carrying out task functions but may give no thought to maintenance functions.

**Group Development.** One of the most familiar group process theories related to maintenance and task functions is that of group development, which is "the maturity and degree of cohesion that a group achieves over time as members interact, learn about one another, and structure relationships and roles within the group" (Mennecke, Hoffer, and Wynne, 1992, p. 526). As they engage in their maintenance and task functions, most learning groups also experience growth and development. Many facilitators and learners are familiar with group development theory because of the work of Tuckman (1965), who developed a model proposing that group behavior progresses through four stages: forming, storming, norming, and performing. In a review and synthesis of group development models, Mennecke, Hoffer, and Wynne (1992) suggest that models display the following common developmental phases: orientation, in which the group develops and refines its purpose and goals; exploration, in which members explore behavioral boundaries; normalization, in which individual roles and norms are established and enforced; production, in which the group develops the type of cohesion that enables it to maximize its task-related behavior; and termination, in which task-related behavior is reduced, while interpersonal behaviors are increased.

A different type of model of group development has been developed by Kasl, Marsick, and Dechant (1992). Based on their research on team learning, they propose that learning groups undergo phases of learning. Using the work of learning theorists such as Jack Mezirow, David Kolb, Peter Jarvis, and Donald Schön, they have developed a model of group learning consisting of four phases: contained learning, collected learning, constructed learning, and continuous learning. According to this model, as the group develops an identity, learning gradually shifts from individual (contained) learning to cooperative (collected) learning to collaborative (constructive) learning, which the group is able to continue on an ongoing basis (continuous learning). As described by Cranton in Chapter Three, however, not all group learning tasks may require reaching the phases of constructed or continuous learning.

In describing their learning model, Dechant, Marsick, and Kasl (1993) acknowledge the influence of group theory but state that what they are portraying as group learning differs from the descriptions of group development in the group dynamics literature because of its emphasis on learning rather than on task achievement (Kasl, Dechant, and Marsick, 1993). Although that is true, the realization of their model depends on a group development process in which members establish relationships and engage in both task and maintenance behaviors. (In Chapter Four, Armstrong and Yarbrough present another model of group development based on their experiences with learning groups.)

**Facilitator's Role.** In dividing a class into learning subgroups, the facilitator may decide to spend little time discussing how the work of the groups will be carried out, focusing instead on the learning task. While such an approach makes sense for short-term ad hoc groups, in ongoing groups, "the personal and working relationships within the small group can either make or break the course experience for many [learners]" (Miller, Trimbur, and Wilkes, 1994, p. 34). Therefore, some attention to group process is required. In their work with collaborative learning groups in an undergraduate biology course, Miller, Trimbur, and Wilkes (1994) found that "initially . . . the process-related issue of group dynamics consumed as much or more faculty effort than issues related to content."

Our experience working with learning groups has also demonstrated the need to attend to group process. In facilitating a seminar, "Race and Gender in Adult Education," Susan Imel naively assumed that the subgroups could run the course with little or no interference from her. Although the subgroups were quite capable of handling task functions, it soon became clear that time should be devoted to other aspects of group process, especially issues related to power. After Susan facilitated two discussions of group process, members of the class assumed responsibility for this task.

Although the facilitator may have a role in preparing individuals for group work and helping them process their group experiences, both Knights (1993) and Foley (1992) warn against taking on group maintenance functions. By being overly supportive and assuming the role of caretaker, facilitators fail to challenge learners to take responsibility for their own learning.

**Forming Groups.** In forming learning subgroups, the facilitator is faced with a number of questions, including what size groups should be and whether learners should select their own groups. Size is an important characteristic of groups. According to Levine and Moreland (1990, p. 596), "studies on the sizes of natural groups suggest that people strongly prefer smaller groups." Jaques (1991) and Zander (1994) both point out that the size of a group has a bearing on its other characteristics. Smaller groups, those of six or less, tend to be more cohesive and productive than larger groups. Even in a class of eight to twelve learners, therefore, group theory indicates that forming two small subgroups might produce better results for some purposes.

Because it is a common practice in adult education to form smaller subgroups within the context of a larger group, facilitators must be aware of the relationship between the small groups and the large group, which Knights (1993) calls "the intergroup effect." In commenting on his experiences with small groups, Knights (p. 193) observes that even though learners develop a great deal of comfort in their small groups, some find the whole group environment to be "a dangerous place," and some also encounter a "feeling that they are missing out on an experience that has been happening elsewhere." By alerting learners to the existence of the intergroup phenomenon, facilitators can reduce its negative impact.

Although theory speaks conclusively about the importance of size, it is not so explicit about the question of learners choosing or being assigned to groups. In naturally occurring groups, members tend to share similarities, and "many groups recruit new members primarily through social networks of friends and relatives" (Levine and Moreland, 1990, p. 597). Because of the voluntary nature of adult education and because many of the participants in her classes are already acquainted, Susan has always allowed learners to form their own subgroups, suggesting only that these groups consist of no more than six members. Although the decisions about subgroup membership are supposedly made on the basis of topic, she assumes that some learners use the criterion of who else is going to be in the group.

Miller, Trimbur, and Wilkes (1994) describe quite a different approach to forming the collaborative learning subgroups in their undergraduate biology classes. Having found that diversity among group members increases performance, they administer the Myers-Briggs Type Indicator and Gordon's cognitive topology to assess learners' personality and cognitive types and use the results as a basis for creating heterogeneous groups. Even though it makes reaching consensus more difficult, Kasl, Dechant, and Marsick (1993) are also advocates for heterogeneous groups because they believe that diverse perspectives can enhance group learning.

**Addressing Power and Conflict.** Clearly, an important issue for adult educators is how to deal with conflict and examine and attend to power relations in groups. While there is some discussion of dealing with group conflict in the group relations literature (for example, Levine and Moreland, 1990), most of this literature is based on the theoretical underpinnings of humanistic psychology. Foley (1992) notes that in general, the literature dealing with group relations with respect to adult education is based on a combination of instrumentalism, which tends to deal with a group's task functions, and humanistic psychology, which focuses more on the maintenance functions of the group. He argues that "the instrumentalist/humanistic approach to teaching and group work can lead to group leaders adopting a 'false self' of endlessly supportive facilitator, and to the development of a style of teaching and learning that ignores unconscious motivations and responses, and which does not challenge and extend learners" (Foley, 1992, p. 143).

This instrumentalist and humanistic psychology approach that has been prevalent in the field of adult education has dealt with the issue of conflict in groups, primarily from the standpoint of how the facilitator can be supportive of individual group members, and thus the group as a whole, in order to help the group resolve conflict, move beyond it, and get on with the task functions. According to this view, conflict is seen primarily as being generated from personality factors and differing life experiences among members. Those from the Tavistock school (Bion as cited by Foley, 1992) move beyond a humanistic psychology-instrumentalist orientation and employ psychoanalytic constructs, including the mechanisms of transference, countertransference, and unconscious projection of fantasy from one member to another, both to explain and resolve group conflict.

Whereas the role of unconscious projection is no doubt at play in groups, what is missing in the group relations literature—and the adult education literature that relies on it—is attention to power relations based on structural systems of privilege and oppression such as gender, race, class, and sexual orientation, and how these structural factors contribute to understandings of conflict and overall group process. Lack of attention to structural factors is due, in part, to the fact that the theoretical underpinnings of the group relations in adult education literature (humanistic psychology-instrumentalism-psychoanalysis) tend to ignore these structural factors. Recognizing these limitations, Knights (1993, p. 195) notes that "it is in this area . . . that group relations theory has much to learn from work that has in recent years become current in literary and cultural studies." Literary and cultural studies, as well as critical and feminist theory and pedagogy, make power relations based on structural factors such as race, ethnicity, gender, and sexual orientation more apparent because their units of analysis are either these structural factors or the connections between the individual and these structural factors.

In spite of the fact that most of the adult education literature that relates to teaching and group work is based largely on a humanistic psychology perspective, there is a developing body of literature based on various types of critical, feminist, Africentric, or poststructural theory relative to different aspects of adult education (see for example, Brookfield, 1995; Cervero and Wilson,

1994; Hart, 1992; Hayes and Colin, 1994; Sheared, 1994; Tisdell, 1993, 1995; Welton, 1995). However, there has been little merging of these bodies of adult education literature with the group relations literature. The adult education literature, with these more critically oriented theoretical frames as a base, deals specifically with power relations based on the structural factors of race, gender, class, and so on. Thus, it more specifically addresses the "challenge" factor in the role of facilitator that Foley (1992) suggests has been ignored in favor of the adoption of the role of "endlessly supportive facilitator." Even though most are concerned that acknowledging or addressing these factors in groups will lead to conflict, adult educators need to consider how power relations based on these structural factors are manifested in both entire classroom groups and smaller subgroups and how they might be dealt with while attending to the task and maintenance functions of the group. Perhaps an example from Libby Tisdell's master's-level class, "Transformational Leadership in Adult Education," will illustrate issues of power relations and conflict within an entire classroom group.

As the instructor and group facilitator, Libby had a task function of introducing students to different theories of leadership and their relationship to adult education leadership practices in a variety of contexts. Eighteen students (two women of color, the rest white) were enrolled in the class. One day, a discussion of leadership issues in distance education resulted in a conflictual exchange within the group. The most privileged (by race, class, and professional status) members of the class were two white women. In part because of their class and professional status privilege, they had the most knowledge of technology and the most access to it, and they also had a good deal of power and persuasive ability in the group. They argued that organizations providing educational services need to be using computers and other technology in education, because in this information age it is the wave of the future and those who do not use technology will be in a disadvantaged position. The two women of color (one African American, the other Native American) raised the issue of who has access to such technology and for what kinds of learning, and the importance of relationship and connection (the role of community) in learning. In response, the two white women espoused the merits of "listservs" and "chat groups" on the Internet in meeting relational needs. The Native American woman explained in an exasperated tone that efforts were being made to use educational technology on a local Indian reservation with very little attention to the cultural needs of the community, ending by saying, "And they aren't going to use it!"

Recognizing that the group was in conflict, Libby felt obliged to intervene as the facilitator and to point out the class and cultural issues underlying the discussion, particularly the issues raised by the women of color. The issue of access to technology has class implications, whereas the issues of the types of learning and the role of connection, relationship, and the importance of community in learning are partly cultural issues, particularly for communities that believe knowledge is in the community and not in a box (the computer).

Because several authors have discussed the importance of connection and relationship in women's learning, they are also gender issues. In an effort to keep the group on task in relationship to leadership issues, Libby pointed out these underlying class, gender, and cultural issues and highlighted the importance of considering such issues in leadership issues in adult education. But in an effort to also tend to the maintenance function of the group, she wanted to validate and affirm the contributions of both factions. She asked how leaders in distance education might take into account the cultural needs of communities that believe knowledge is in the community and not in a box, and also use computers.

Libby recognized that it was the women of color in particular who raised the issues noted. Given their own membership in nondominant cultural groups, they were more attuned to these important issues often overlooked by white leaders in distance education. Because comments by those marginalized by more systems of oppression are often discounted in subtle but significant (and mostly unconscious) ways (Tisdell, 1993, 1995), Libby thought it particularly important to highlight the importance of the underlying issues being raised. The students in the class also tended to defer to these white women, due to their professional status, experience, and their class and race privilege. Yet it is was important to acknowledge the value of what they were contributing to the discussion. Whereas no direct discussion occurred about power relations in the group and their reflection of power relations in society, reframing the discussion in this way highlighted how these issues are always at play and how they affect leadership decisions and the task and maintenance aspects of this and all groups. Whereas Libby's strategy seemed to resolve this particular group conflict, the situation could have been handled in other ways. No intervention, however, could have led to more conflict in the group and diverted the group from its main task of exploring leadership issues in adult education.

## Conclusion

The adult education literature has tended to treat the topic of learning in groups as a subtext rather than as a main theme. Although the group dynamics literature has contributed much to the development of adult learning groups, knowledge from other areas can also enhance learning groups. As demonstrated by Kasl, Marsick, and Dechant (1992), the relationship between group process theory and learning theory needs further exploration. Also, to understand issues related to power, adult educators need to look beyond theories of group process and group behavior based on humanistic psychology or with an instrumentalist orientation. Knights (1993) suggests learning from recent work in literacy and cultural studies that encourages "an understanding of text as a weave of voices, as dialogue, as the site of inconsistency and contradiction" (p. 195). Finally, Foley (1992, p. 158) warns against "fall[ing] into the instrumentalist fallacy . . . that the practitioner can acquire a comprehensive model by which to work, or can develop a kitbag of techniques and produce the appropriate one as needed." Our experiences working with groups have demonstrated that too many factors lie outside our influence for us to attempt to control their outcomes. Yet reflecting on our practice and its relationship to theory has enabled us to continue to enhance the experiences of learning groups.

## References

Brookfield, S. D. *Becoming a Critically Reflective Teacher.* San Francisco: Jossey-Bass, 1995.
Cervero, R. M., and Wilson, A. L. *Planning Responsibly for Adult Education: A Guide to Negotiating Power and Interests.* San Francisco: Jossey-Bass, 1994.
Cragan, J. F., and Wright, D. W. *Communication in Small Group Discussions: An Integrated Approach.* (3rd ed.) St. Paul, Minn.: West, 1991.
Dechant, K., Marsick, V. J., and Kasl, E. "Towards a Model of Team Learning." *Studies in Continuing Education,* 1993, *15* (1), 1–14.
Foley, G. "Going Deeper: Teaching and Group Work in Adult Education." *Studies in the Education of Adults,* 1992, *24* (2), 143–161.
Hart, M. *Working and Educating for Life: Feminist and International Perspectives on Adult Education.* New York: Routledge, 1992.
Hayes, E., and Colin, S.A.J., III (eds.). *Confronting Racism and Sexism.* New Directions for Adult and Continuing Education, no. 61. San Francisco: Jossey-Bass, 1994.
Jaques, D. *Learning in Groups.* (2nd ed.) London: Kogan Page, 1991.
Kasl, E., Dechant, K., and Marsick, V. "Living the Learning: Internalizing Our Model of Group Learning." In D. Boud, R. Cohen, and D. Walker (eds.), *Using Experience for Learning.* Bristol, Pa.: Society for Research into Higher Education and Open University Press, 1993.
Kasl, E., Marsick, V., and Dechant, K. "A Conceptual Model for Group Learning." In A. Blount (ed.), *Annual Adult Education Research Conference (AERC). Proceedings (33rd, Saskatoon, Saskatchewan, Canada, May 15–17, 1992).* (Rev. ed.) Saskatoon: College of Education, University of Saskatchewan, 1992. (ED 368 856)
Knights, B. "Hearing Yourself Teach: Group Processes for Adult Educators." *Studies in the Education of Adults,* 1993, *25* (2), 184–198.
Levine, J. M., and Moreland, R. L. "Progress in Small Group Research." In M. R. Rosenzweig and L. W. Porter (eds.), *Annual Review of Psychology.* Vol. 41. Palo Alto, Calif.: Annual Reviews, 1990.
Mennecke, B. E., Hoffer, J. A., and Wynne, B. E. "The Implications of Group Development and History for Group Support System Theory and Practice." *Small Group Research,* 1992, *23* (4), 524–572.
Miller, J. E., Trimbur, J., and Wilkes, J. M. "Group Dynamics: Understanding Group Success and Failure in Collaborative Learning." In K. Bosworth and S. J. Hamilton (eds.), *Collaborative Learning: Underlying Processes and Effective Techniques.* New Directions for Teaching and Learning, no. 59. San Francisco: Jossey-Bass, 1994.
Sheared, V. "Giving Voice: An Inclusive Model of Instruction—A Womanist Perspective." In E. Hayes and S.A.J. Colin III (eds.), *Confronting Racism and Sexism.* New Directions for Adult and Continuing Education, no. 61. San Francisco: Jossey-Bass, 1994.
Tisdell, E. "Interlocking Systems of Power, Privilege, and Oppression in Adult Higher Education Classes." *Adult Education Quarterly,* 1993, *43* (4), 203–226.
Tisdell, E. *Creating Inclusive Adult Learning Environments: Insights from Multicultural Education and Feminist Pedagogy.* In no. 361. Columbus: ERIC Clearinghouse on Adult, Career,

and Vocational Education, Center on Education and Training for Employment, College of Education, Ohio State University, 1995.

Tuckman, B. W. "Developmental Sequence in Small Groups." *Psychological Bulletin*, 1965, 63, 384–399.

Welton, M. (ed.). *In Defense of the Lifeworld: Critical Perspectives on Adult Education.* New York: State University of New York Press, 1995.

Zander, A. *Making Groups Effective.* (2nd ed.) San Francisco: Jossey-Bass, 1994.

SUSAN IMEL *is director of the ERIC Clearinghouse on Adult, Career, and Vocational Education and adjunct assistant professor in the College of Education, The Ohio State University.*

ELIZABETH J. TISDELL *is a core faculty member at Antioch University, Seattle.*

*We use group work every day in our practice—but what kinds of groups and for what purpose? This chapter distinguishes among three types of groups and relates each to the domain of learning it promotes.*

# Types of Group Learning

*Patricia Cranton*

That group work is a valuable strategy has become an unquestioned tenet of our practice. In every classroom of adult learners, we expect to see groups of people working happily and harmoniously on group activities. As a result of this expectation, educators in all varieties of settings and contexts are likely to be advising their learners: "Form groups of four or five individuals, discuss, and try to come to consensus on. . . ." But what is group learning? Why do we use it? What type of learning does it promote? Do different types of groups lead to different kinds of learning? The history, foundations, and nature of groups are discussed in Chapter One and Chapter Two. In this chapter, I contend that there are distinct types of groups, each emerging from varying learner needs, interests, and contexts and each leading to unique kinds of knowledge.

The terms used to describe types of groups can be overlapping, confusing, and contradictory. We hear about cooperation, work teams, collaboration, quality circles, and participatory learning, to name but a few of the popular expressions. Following as much as is possible the terminology used in the adult education literature (for example, Imel, 1991), I distinguish between *cooperative, collaborative,* and *transformative* group learning. As a foundation for this distinction, I draw on Habermas's (1971) three domains of human interests and knowledge. For each type of group, I describe its special characteristics, the nature of the learning goals, and the roles of the educator.

## Kinds of Human Interests and Knowledge

Given that there is little research on the nature of learning groups, I base my discussion on a well-respected philosophical framework. Habermas (1971) and those who follow his thinking (for example, Mezirow, 1991) describe people as having three basic interests, each of which leads them to acquire a different kind of knowledge. First, we are interested in ways to control and manipulate our environment so as to have such things as shelter, food, and transportation. Through this interest, we accumulate *instrumental knowledge*—scientific, cause-and-effect information. Second, we want to understand each other and the social norms of the context within which we live and work. In order to do this, we obtain *communicative knowledge*—mutual understanding and social knowledge. Third, we have a basic interest in our own personal growth and development, including freedom from the constraints of not knowing. This desire can lead us to *emancipatory knowledge*—increased self-awareness and transformation of our perspectives.

Having the acquisition of different kinds of knowledge as a learning goal can lead to quite distinct types of groups. A group of nursing students struggling to understand the intricacies of medications might be seeking instrumental knowledge. In a leadership development workshop series where participants are learning about and practicing conflict resolution strategies, the goal is likely to be communicative learning. In a self-help group for bereaved parents, individuals may experience emancipatory learning.

## Cooperative Group Learning

Although cooperation and collaboration are synonyms in dictionaries, they have come to have dissimilar connotations for those writing about group learning. Cooperative learning, as advocated in the literature on teaching children (for example, Slavin, 1986), is a structured process that requires learners to work together on a task, share information, and encourage and support each other. The emphasis is on cooperating to get a task accomplished. The successful completion of the task involves or leads to the acquisition of knowledge about the subject matter. It is usually suggested that group skills are learned in advance or separately from the subject matter.

When group learning is used for the acquisition of instrumental knowledge, the cooperative group is most appropriate. Instrumental knowledge is objective, rational, definitive, and scientific. The issues are clear cut or black and white. Instrumental knowledge is established through empirical validation rather than through discourse. In cooperative group learning, the focus of the learning is on the subject matter rather than on the interpersonal process. At the same time, the strengths, experiences, and expertise of individual group members can contribute to the learning of the group as a whole.

A group of learners in a safety training program in an industrial shop could, for example, work with a fairly structured set of tasks in which they compile and update the various shop regulations related to safety in their division. Each person has experience with different aspects of the operation and can provide information as to the relevance of existing procedures and regulations. Through cooperative and experiential learning, individuals would be more likely to learn about total shop safety than if they simply read or listened to the information.

To give an illustration where the subject area is less structured, students working in cooperative groups in a statistics course can encourage and support each other. Those who have a facility with mathematics or computers can offer that expertise to the group as they work through a set of data analysis exercises.

Cooperative group learning is becoming the backbone of distance education (for example, Main and Berry, 1993). It is appropriate and popular in military education, health professions education, and in most technical training. Some authors argue that cooperative learning can be applicable to any subject through the use of different group structures for specific tasks (Kagan, 1993). However, in many instances, the distinction between cooperative and collaborative group learning is blurred, and what is called cooperative could perhaps be better viewed as collaborative (see Simpson, 1995, for an example).

In cooperative group learning, the educator designs the exercises, activities, experiences, or problems that the learners work through. They may be quite structured, including objectives, time constraints, detailed formats for the presentation of products, and perhaps evaluation guidelines. During group learning, the educator manages the time and resources, checks that the work is progressing satisfactorily, and intercedes when a group is going off-task. In this role, the educator remains an expert, keeps position power, and is in control of the process of evaluation.

## Collaborative Group Learning

Collaborative learning is shared inquiry (MacGregor, 1990). In other words, individuals work together to construct knowledge rather than to discover objective truths. Imel (1991) points out that in collaborative learning, we assume that knowledge is socially produced by communities or groups and that anyone can participate in the process of shaping and testing ideas. People exchange ideas, feelings, experiences, information, and insights and through this exchange come to an understanding that is acceptable to all group members. The emphasis is, in large part, on the process—listening to and respecting others, understanding alternative perspectives, challenging and questioning others, negotiating points of view, and caring for both the individuals and the group as a whole. Farquharson (1995, p. 63) describes the "kind of mutual affirmation" of perspectives that occurs in a collaborative group and the way that "similar experiences contribute to the construction of like meanings that are not readily understood by the outsider."

Communicative knowledge (Habermas, 1971; Mezirow, 1991) is a knowledge of social norms, traditions, and values underlying our culture, and a mutual understanding among individuals. Human beings living together in a family, organization, community, society, or culture, need to rely on each other and get along with each other for all to survive and have a meaningful life. Habermas calls this a "practical" human interest. What we do is agree upon ways of living together. We have laws and norms of behavior. For example, in the larger social units of societies and cultures, we have commonly agreed upon legal systems and religious affiliations that guide our ways of being together. We may agree that taking each other's property is wrong; we may agree that marriage is sacred. In subcultures, the mutual understanding may be counter to the mainstream cultural norms. Violence against others may be seen as an indication of courage or manliness. Having more than one mate may be seen as a sign of holding a liberal viewpoint. In smaller social units, such as families and organizations, we also come to agreement on what we value. We may agree that everyone in the family shares household duties; we may agree that everyone in the organization values teamwork. All such knowledge is communicative—it is based on the use of language to come to agreement. The knowledge is valid when all members of the group are in accord. What is valid knowledge in one group may not be valid knowledge in another group; hence different countries have different legal, social, and educational systems, and different religions have different interpretations of morality.

When the learning goal is the acquisition of communicative knowledge, collaborative groups are most appropriate. It is here that the diversity of individuals' experiences, ideas, values, and insights can be brought together to come to an understanding of the nature of human interactions. For example, in a professional development seminar on divorce arbitration for counselors, group members can share strategies and stories and interpret each others' experiences, thereby adding to their understanding. Learners are more likely to gain meaningful new perspectives on the issues than if they listened to one expert's view on how to conduct arbitration. The process of the counselors' getting to know each other and developing as a group contributes significantly to their learning—their shared construction of meaning. Process and content are inseparable here, unlike cooperative group learning in which the content is the primary focus.

In many diverse subject areas, collaborative group learning is appropriate for the nature of the knowledge we want to acquire. Whenever we are interested in how people relate to each other and develop social realities, it is communicative knowledge we are seeking. This is the domain of the social sciences, including psychology, sociology, and politics. It is the territory of administrative studies, such as leadership, organizational behavior, and management. Literacy programs (Hayes and Walter, 1995), counseling groups, and discussion groups or study circles (see Oliver, 1995, for a clear description of study circles as collaborative learning) are all contexts within which collaborative groups are meaningful.

In practice, and in spite of adult education rhetoric to the contrary, many educators have difficulties with the concept of socially constructed knowledge. We tend to see our own disciplines as containing objective facts, of being empirically verifiable. We are not inclined to question the premises and assumptions underlying our area of expertise. Therefore, we think, collaborative learning in which knowledge is *constructed* is not appropriate—it is better that we tell the learners what the facts are, and then they can discuss the issues once they are informed. Jarvis (1992, p. 31) explains this phenomenon well when he writes, "People create and habitualize their actions, and these actions then assume the appearance of objective reality. Other people tend to accept the objectivity of the culture into which they are socialized." We learn the language of our culture or any social unit (for example, our family or organization) and consider it to be value free. We conform to social norms as if they were objective. However, it is through collaborative group learning and the consequent introduction of new perspectives from group members that we may be able to see the sources and consequences of our communicative knowledge.

The role of the educator in collaborative group learning can be confusing and perhaps troublesome. The educator establishes an atmosphere or climate in which collaboration is possible. There must be a democratic environment in which people respect and listen to each other. The educator is to be an equal participant in the shared inquiry, yet also responsible for facilitating and maintaining the process. Authority and power over the group need to be given up, yet the educator is relied on to help group members work collaboratively. The educator is described as being accountable for preparing materials, problems, activities, and clear outcomes (for example, see MacGregor, 1990), but at the same time is a co-learner. There is a delicate balance to be sustained here, perhaps an impossible one in some contexts. Educators working with collaborative group learning must be very clear about their own conceptualization of collaboration, be critically reflective about their practice, and be exceptionally sensitive to the nature of the group process.

## Transformative Group Learning

Transformative learning occurs when people revise their underlying expectations, assumptions, or perspectives. The process may be prompted by a life experience or dilemma, either positive or negative. It may also be stimulated by new perspectives encountered in a learning group or through reading. The learner is led to critically reflect on his or her assumptions or habitual expectations—the notion that "this is the way things are because this is the way I have always seen them to be." If the assumptions, or "meaning schemes" as Mezirow (1991) calls them, are found to be invalid in the light of the new experience, the learner may decide to revise them. When a whole set of interrelated meaning schemes is revised, the individual has made a shift in a meaning perspective.

Transformative learning empowers individuals, as options and alternative ways of seeing the world become available. If I do not know there is a choice, I am less free. Transformative group learning promotes the empowerment of learners; the goal is freedom from the constraint of not knowing. This type of group learning has also been called participatory (Hayes and Walter, 1995), but I choose the term transformative, seeing it as more descriptive of the process involved.

In transformative group learning, individuals take responsibility for their own learning. They seek out new perspectives, challenge commonly held views, question themselves and each other, and often work toward change outside of the group or program. Learners may identify problems and constraints that they share, define collective goals, and engage in group action to address their concerns. The focus may be on epistemic perspectives (knowledge-based) if learners are working in the same profession or subject area. It may be on sociolinguistic perspectives (social norms and the use of language) if people share a concern with a social issue, such as sexism or racism; or the emphasis may be on psychological perspectives if the individuals are working toward a common personal goal—recovering from an abusive relationship, for example.

Emancipatory knowledge can be described as freedom from "libidinal, linguistic, epistemic, institutional, or environmental forces that limit our options and our rational control over our lives but have been taken for granted or seen as beyond human control" (Mezirow, 1991, p. 87). People have a basic interest in their own growth and development. They wish to be free from self-distortions and social distortions of knowledge. Few would choose to be oppressed, manipulated, powerless, or helpless upon knowing that there was a choice, and if they did, we would argue that this was a product of a limiting psychological perspective. The fundamental desire to improve oneself is evident in the popularity of self-help books, workshops, and programs on enhancing almost every aspect of our lives.

When the goal of a group is emancipatory learning, transformative group learning best describes the process. Individuals who are seeking to change their practice or careers, community groups who want to address environmental issues, or people who are dealing with personally traumatic experiences all have empowerment as a learning goal and will best be able to move toward that goal by critically questioning current expectations and perspectives. The process is collaborative, but it goes beyond mutual understanding and has as a goal to effect change, either individually or socially.

I will provide an illustration from my own practice. I work with groups of graduate students who are, or who are interested in becoming, adult educators. They have a variety of experiences in the field and educational backgrounds that always include participation in traditional university programs. I introduce self-directed learning, both in theory and, more gradually, in practice. Over two semesters, I expect participants to take increasing responsibility for their own learning, and I withdraw from making decisions about topics, exercises, or evaluation. I encourage critical self-reflection through journals, case studies, and critical incidents, although I never assign such activities. This experience challenges the expectations that learners have of both the educator and the learner roles. There may be anxiety, anger, and resistance. As the group forms and becomes collaborative, individuals question their own and each other's perspectives on educational practice. Some people choose not to change their assumptions or their practice, but many do revise the way they see their work.

Transformative group learning occurs in many contexts. Individual transformative learning may take place in counseling groups, literacy education, professional development workshops, or weight loss and fitness programs, to give but a few examples. When social change is a goal, we may see transformative learning in community action groups, environmental groups, political networks, women's groups, or labor education groups.

The role of the educator in transformative group learning varies over time. As I describe in detail elsewhere (Cranton, 1994, 1996), the educator begins the process by giving up position power (formal authority and control) but maintaining and using personal power (expertise, authenticity, and loyalty). Equal participation in discourse is encouraged, and learner decision making is promoted. This sets the stage for critical self-refection. When an atmosphere of comfort and collaboration is established, the educator's role becomes one of stimulating reflection through critical questioning and consciousness-raising activities such as role playing, simulations, and journal writing. Using experiential techniques and critical incidents can also be helpful. It is essential that the educator not impose his or her own perspectives on learners but rather encourage individuals to question their own perspectives. Equally important to challenging learners is the provision of support. Questioning one's assumptions can be disconcerting or even painful. The educator should remain authentic and trustworthy, foster group members' support of each other, and encourage networks both within and outside of the group itself. Conflict must be handled with care, and support must be available for personal adjustments and for those individuals who choose to act on changes they make as a result of the group's work.

It is much easier to write about the educator's roles in transformative group learning than it is to implement them in practice. Most of us feel discomfort in giving up position power, for example, and we worry about the reactions of colleagues or program administrators to our unorthodox approach to teaching. To become a truly equal participant in the group process is to feel vulnerable as an educator. Perhaps the roles evolve best with confidence in what one is doing and experience in doing it well.

## Conclusion

In this chapter, I describe three types of group learning, each leading to a different kind of knowledge acquisition. In cooperative group learning, individuals share information and expertise in order to work together on a task. The emphasis is on the task rather than the process, and the experience is fairly structured. The educator remains in control of the content and the process. I argue that this type of group work is most productive when obtaining instrumental knowledge is the goal.

In collaborative group learning, individuals work together to construct their own understanding of each other and their social world. The emphasis is on the process and the interactions among the people involved. The educator establishes the atmosphere in which such inquiry is possible and participates in the shared exploration. Collaborative group learning yields communicative knowledge.

In transformative group learning, group members engage in critical reflection in order to examine their expectations, assumptions, and perspectives about the world around them. The goal is increased self-awareness and empowerment through consciousness raising. Individual and social change may both be goals of transformative group learning. The educator establishes an environment conducive to critical reflection, stimulates the process, and ensures that learners are supported. Transformative group learning leads to emancipatory knowledge.

## References

Cranton, P. *Understanding and Promoting Transformative Learning: A Guide for Educators of Adults.* San Francisco: Jossey-Bass, 1994.

Cranton, P. *Professional Development as Transformative Learning: New Perspectives for Teachers of Adults.* San Francisco: Jossey-Bass, 1996.

Farquharson, A. *Teaching in Practice: How Professionals Can Work Effectively with Clients, Patients, and Colleagues.* San Francisco: Jossey-Bass, 1995.

Habermas, J. *Human Interests and Knowledge.* Boston: Beacon Press, 1971.

Hayes, E., and Walter, P. G. "A Comparison of Small Group Learning Approaches in Adult Literacy Education." *Adult Basic Education,* 1995, 5 (3), 133–151.

Imel, S. *Collaborative Learning in Adult Education.* ERIC Digest no. 113. Columbus: ERIC Clearinghouse on Adult, Career, and Vocational Education, Center on Education and Training for Employment, Ohio State University, 1991.

Jarvis, P. *Paradoxes of Learning: On Becoming an Individual in Society.* San Francisco: Jossey-Bass, 1992.

Kagan, S. "The Structural Approach to Cooperative Learning." In D. Holt (ed.), *Cooperative Learning: A Response to Linguistic and Cultural Diversity.* McHenry, Ill.: Center for Applied Linguistics and Delta Systems, 1993.

MacGregor, J. "Collaborative Learning: Shared Inquiry as a Process of Reform." In M. D. Svinicki (ed.), *The Changing Face of College Teaching.* New Directions for Teaching and Learning, no. 42. San Francisco: Jossey-Bass, 1990.

Main, C., and Berry, M. "Technology and Education." *Adult Learning,* 1993, 4 (3), 10–11.

Mezirow, J. *Transformative Dimensions of Adult Learning.* San Francisco: Jossey-Bass, 1991.

Oliver, L. P. "Is the United States Ready for a Study Circle Movement?" *Adult Learning,* 1995, 6 (4), 14–16, 19.

Simpson, G. W. "Cooperative Learning with Adults." *Adult Learning,* 1995, 6 (4), 10–11.

Slavin, R. *Using Student Team Learning.* (3rd ed.) Baltimore: Center for Research on Elementary and Middle Schools, Johns Hopkins University, 1986.

*PATRICIA CRANTON is professor of adult education at Brock University in Ontario, Canada.*

*Three central tenets of the group learning process are presented for facilitators and participants to consider as they engage in group learning.*

# Group Learning: The Role of Environment

*Joseph L. Armstrong, Sharon L. Yarbrough*

Until recently, many adult educators may have considered the term *group learning* to be an oxymoron. The traditional view of learning holds that learning is the acquisition of knowledge and that knowledge resides within individuals. Therefore, groups do not learn, individuals do. While the notion that knowledge resides within individuals is debatable, we will not take up this debate here. Instead, we will write from the well-established social constructivist position that knowledge is constructed through social interaction (Berger, 1996), regardless of where it resides. Given this view of knowledge construction, the process of knowledge construction in groups—group learning—becomes a valuable topic of study, one to which the field of adult education has recently begun to return (see Kasl, Marsick, and Dechant, 1992; Imel, 1991).

As interest in group learning grows, those wishing to facilitate group learning look to the literature for models and information. What they find is often inappropriate or inadequate. For example, much of the group development literature from social psychology (Palazzolo, 1981) is attractive, that is, it has much to say to facilitators of group learning. But it is of limited value in at least two ways. First, it treats groups as isolated phenomena, ignoring the fact that groups are not wholly independently functioning units but are institutionally and socially situated. Further, this literature is primarily concerned with the psychosocial functioning of the group and its members, not with learning. Other facilitators of group learning turn to the literature of organizational learning but find it equally lacking. While this literature better acknowledges that groups are institutionally and socially situated, it treats learning primarily as that which furthers organizational goals (Kofman and Senge,

1993), neglecting most of the learning that occurs in groups. Clearly, adult educators wishing to facilitate group learning need additional information.

As facilitators of group learning in business and higher education, we find that three central tenets of group learning are often overlooked, both in practice and in the literature. Hence, much group learning is less than ideal. First, in order for any group learning to occur, the collection of individuals must become a group by developing and maintaining an internal group environment. At the minimum, group members must acquire a rudimentary understanding of one another and of themselves as a group before they can learn any content effectively. They must also have some understanding of how they can develop and function as a group. In other words, learning content alone is insufficient; group members must learn about themselves, their role in the group, and the group's development if effective group learning is to occur.

The second tenet is related to the group's position within a larger institutional and social milieu. Learning groups do not function in a vacuum but are situated within a larger context that continually influences the group's actions. The group, however, is not merely a passive recipient of institutional influence but can influence and reshape the larger institutional and social contexts within which it resides. The group and the institution are engaged in a continuously reciprocal relationship (as are the group and its individual members).

The last overlooked tenet has to do with the perceptions of and about the group. Both members' and outsiders' perceptions of the group affect its functioning. Anyone facilitating or participating in a learning group must continually consider and manage these influences. Drawing from our own experiences working with learning groups, we will illustrate these three concepts and their role in group learning.

## Internal Environment of the Group

A collection of individuals is not necessarily a group. The collection must become a group. We call this process of becoming a group "acquiring an internal group environment"; it has two components: interdependence and group development. The development and maintenance of the internal group environment is the responsibility of all group members. Initially, the facilitator will probably shoulder the majority of this responsibility, but if the group is to be successful, all members must, at different times, assume at least some of the responsibility for the group's internal environment.

Our experience has shown that at least a modicum of attention must be devoted to this environment in order for any group learning to occur. Unless members of the group are aware of and attend to the internal group environment, any learning that occurs will be individual in nature and coincidental to the group. Some indications of internal group environment include group members' growing interdependence and stages of group development.

**Interdependence.** As group participants spend time together, they naturally grow to rely on one another, that is, they develop interdependence. We feel interdependence is so critical to group learning that any learning without it is not group learning at all. Unless group members experience interdependence, they are merely a collection of individuals learning independently along side one another. Group learning occurs when a group of individuals learn in concert with and through each other. To accomplish this, group members must come to know, trust, and depend on each other. Each member must assume responsibility for the learning of other group members as well as for his or her own. Each must share thoughts, feelings, and assumptions so they can be fully understood by others in the group and must strive to understand others just as fully. Only then can group members move beyond the sharing of ideas that normally occurs in learning situations and begin to construct knowledge jointly. In other words, only when group members become interdependent can group learning occur.

**Stages of Group Development.** Another influence on internal group process is the progression through the stages of group development. As discussed in Chapter Two, most models of group development stages come from social psychology. Our experience has shown that none of the existing models fully captures the progression necessary for developing internal group environment in learning groups. Based on our experience as group facilitators, we suggest that those engaged in group learning keep in mind the following five-stage process that seems to capture the stages of development in learning groups.

1. *Politeness.* In the initial stages of group formation, members get acquainted. Society teaches that it is rude to freely express opinions and agendas, so members are reserved and acquiesce to others. At this stage, group members do not say what they believe and do not disagree with others. No significant learning occurs at this stage.

2. *Focus.* In this stage, groups tentatively plan their work. In learning groups, the group's work is learning—which is not as simple as it sounds. Individual group members must negotiate what they intend to learn, how they intend to learn it, and why they feel it is important.

3. *Conflict.* Groups often experience conflict during their development. At least two conflicts emerge during this stage. Individuals struggle to negotiate their place within the group, and the group as a whole struggles to find an identity. Group members ask—often they ask themselves—"What is this group's purpose, and what is my role in that purpose?" And further, "What is your purpose, and how can we reconcile our respective purposes in this group?"

4. *Solidification.* As group members begin to reconcile the many questions from earlier stages, the group becomes more cohesive; members get to know each other better and depend on each other more. At this stage, group learning becomes easier. Group members understand the process and know each other well enough to interact effectively.

5. *Performance.* When it reaches the last stage, the group can function at a highly productive and efficient level. Group learning is most proficient at this stage.

These stages are not as discrete as they appear. Some elements of each stage are present at all times in the group, but the tasks of each stage seem to come to the forefront and consume a disproportionate amount of the group's time in this order. Those facilitating group learning must be aware of these stages and help the group negotiate the potential problems in each that may hinder its learning.

## Context of the Group

The influence of the environment on group learning is complex and needs more consideration. Dimensions of the environment can have an impact on the behavior of the people in the group. Knowledge of the environment helps heighten certain types of behavior to meet the goals of the group.

**Defining Environment.** Arranging environmental conditions to maximize certain behaviors is a challenge the facilitator of the group must meet. As intact social systems, groups have boundaries, with interdependence among members, along with differentiated member and group roles. Boundaries provide parameters to identify systems of interrelationships and patterns and to differentiate what is inside the group from what is outside. At these boundaries, groups continuously interact with the environment (Czander, 1993). Given the complexity of the relationship between groups and the environment, the group cannot be fully understood without knowledge of the environment.

How environments are distinguished provides further understanding of the group environment. The more common classifications of group environment are the *internal environment* and the *external environment*. A detailed description of internal group environment was provided earlier and is defined as *ambiguous dimensions and forces outside the group that may affect it*. How we define environment depends on what we wish to know about it. For instance, if we wanted to understand how a group functioned in a given situation, we would define the environment in terms of the characteristics and manners of that specific group. Here, we define environment as the properties and forces that both influence and are influenced by a collection of people, that is, a group. The group is defined by its position within an institutional and social context.

**Variables Within the Environment.** Awareness of the environment as it pertains to the group has varied but common themes. For example, characteristics of the members provide an understanding of the social environment. These characteristics include average age, ability level, socioeconomic background, and educational attainment. The character of the environment is created by and transmitted through its members. The following descriptions of characteristics (based on Sells, 1963) provide greater insight into these variables:

Background characteristics such as age, gender, and socioeconomic status,
 along with skill characteristics such as ability, experience, and training

External reference characteristics such as biologically defined factors like height, weight, physique, race, and physical abnormalities or injuries

Factors related to geographic position or socioeconomic status, such as rural or urban residence, income, occupational classification, amount of savings, number of dependents, and education

Family and primary or marriage group factors such as legal status, status in the family, and number of children

Group membership factors, including the number of group memberships, types of groups, and the social status of groups.

Individual differences within a group can affect the group process; for example, a disparity in the ages of group members may lead to differences of interpretation on certain issues. In addition, personality dispositions, beliefs, attitudes, values, moods, feelings, states of mind, drives, needs, and expectations are seen as individual differences that influence the group process directly and indirectly.

Group behavior can emerge as the product of the interaction of two sets of variables. Characteristics of the individuals—abilities, skills, and aptitudes—and their cognitive and emotional responsiveness—attitudes, opinions, and beliefs—make up one set of variables. The second set pertains to characteristics of the group situation known as the *external environment*. The group interaction is also influenced by individuals' traditions, customs, and rules, as they play their prescribed social roles.

**Perceptions of the Environment.** Different environments are identifiable by specific properties within them. Each environment has a unique atmosphere that contains certain elements. For instance, physical, ecological, organizational, and social environments describe the setting of the group. The physical environment is described by the size of the group and its demographics; the ecological environment includes climate and geographic makeup; the organizational environment is the hierarchical makeup and structural composition of the group; and the social environment relates to group behavior.

Whereas each environment can be perceived as a single entity, each environment may also include properties of other distinctive environments. That is, the physical properties are certainly evident in a particular environment, as well as the social properties of the same environment. In this chapter, we focus our attention primarily on the organizational and social environments, while acknowledging that the overlapping of the environmental properties adds dimensions to the already interesting role of environment in group learning.

## Perceptions of the Group

Efforts to examine the relationship between members of the learning group and the environment have been minimal. The value in analyzing this relationship is that it provides insight into group learning as a process as well as an outcome. One of the primary roles of facilitators of group learning is to assess the effects of environment on the learning group and the members' perceptions of this effect. Accurate assessment can help the group understand its own functioning and thus help its members learn more effectively. Here, we present an example of one such assessment.

The Group Environment Scale (GES) measures the dimensions of a social environment (see Moos, 1979). In a study conducted at a large southeastern medical center, the GES was used to examine the actual and preferred group environment, as perceived by the participants (Yarbrough, 1995). The medical center, composed of a university hospital and a graduate school of medicine, provides patient care in a state-of-the-art setting, comprehensive training for future health professionals, and extensive biomedical research. A random sample of 355 employees was selected from the 4,300 employees at the medical center. One hundred and thirty-six employees responded to the survey.

Study participants rated their actual (current) group environment and their preferred (ideal) group environment. Results showed that participants strongly preferred a different group environment from the one in which they were currently working. The top five characteristics of their preferred or ideal environment were task orientation, order and organization, leader support, independence, and innovation—in contrast to their current environment, which they indicated possessed the following characteristics: anger and aggression, self-discovery, leader control, task orientation, and expressiveness.

Discrepancies between the actual and preferred group climate clearly reflect morale problems and specific areas of dissatisfaction. The very nature of the work in a hospital setting suggests that employees are highly competent. The employees preferred a group environment that would provide them the opportunity to apply their skills and "just do their jobs." The results of the study suggest that changes should occur in the organization and its members in order to bring the actual environment more in line with the one preferred by employees.

In this example, group members' perceptions of the group did not match their expectations. Situations such as this are common in group learning and must be dealt with if the group is to be successful. Information such as that provided by the GES can help facilitators and group members make adjustments necessary for the growth and development of the group, which in turn will enhance the learning of the group.

## Conclusion

The complexity of group learning requires that we not only observe group behavior but that we also observe the environment of the group. The study of group learning becomes the study of the interaction of the group and the environment. Knowledge of group behavior provides a foundation for understanding group learning, but the foundation is not complete unless the environment is taken into account. Developing an awareness of the group's environment becomes a more involved endeavor to focus on the dimensions within which the group functions. This requires that a broader knowledge base be developed, one that reflects a reciprocal perspective that groups are not only influenced by social climate but also that groups cause social climate.

Learning groups do not function in a vacuum. They are socially and institutionally situated. Facilitators and participants of group learning can use the three central tenets discussed in this chapter to better understand and manage their roles in the group and the group's position within the larger social and institutional milieu. Doing so can lead to a more fruitful learning experience for all.

## References

Berger, P. *The Social Construction of Reality: A Treatise in the Sociology of Knowledge.* New York: Doubleday, 1996.

Czander, W. M. *The Psychodynamics of Work and Organizations.* New York: Guilford Press, 1993.

Imel, S. *Collaborative Learning in Adult Education.* ERIC Digest no. 113. Columbus: ERIC Clearinghouse on Adult, Career, and Vocational Education, Center on Education and Training for Employment, Ohio State University, 1991. (ED 334 469)

Kasl, E., Marsick, V., and Dechant, K. "A Conceptual Model for Group Learning." In A. Blount (ed.), *Annual Adult Education Research Conference (AERC). Proceedings (33rd, Saskatoon, Saskatchewan, Canada, May 15–17, 1992).* (Rev. ed.) Saskatoon: College of Education, University of Saskatchewan, 1992. (ED 368 856)

Kofman, F., and Senge, P. "Communities of Commitment: The Heart of Learning Organizations." *Organizational Dynamics,* 1993, 22 (2), 5–23.

Moos, R. H. *Evaluating Educational Environments: Procedures, Measures, Findings, and Policy Implications.* San Francisco: Jossey-Bass, 1979.

Palazzolo, C. *Small Groups: An Introduction.* Belmont, Calif.: Litton, 1981.

Sells, S. "Dimensions of Stimulus Situations Which Account for Behavioral Variance." In *Stimulus Determinants of Behavior.* New York: Ronald Press, 1963.

Yarbrough, S. "The Perceptions of Thinking Styles and Group Environment Among Adults." Unpublished doctoral dissertation, Leadership Studies, College of Education, University of Tennessee, Knoxville, 1995.

JOSEPH L. ARMSTRONG *is research associate at the Institute of Assessment and Evaluation, College of Education, University of Tennessee, Knoxville.*

SHARON L. YARBROUGH *is assistant director, Institute of Assessment and Evaluation, College of Education, University of Tennessee, Knoxville.*

*The author explores methods used with groups and discusses the process of constructing activities that focus on group learning.*

# Constructing Group Learning

*Joe E. Heimlich*

Adopted by an educational association in 1897, the Pedagogic Creed carries a powerful lesson for adult education at the end of the twentieth century: "the educational process has two sides—one psychological and one sociological . . . neither can be subordinated to the other or neglected without evil results following" (Dworkin, 1959). Although some may question the idea of evil results, learning is an individual choice and action, and education is in part a social process conceived as a continuously sustained effort of humanity to build on the past for the future (Lawson, 1961). Multiple roles, values, and levels of expertise exist in any group of adult learners (Lovell, 1987). Taken together, these ideas suggest that a group of individuals can function either as a single learning unit or as several subgroups and that educators of adults are well served in exploring ways to use groups and subgroups more effectively. Further, the ways in which individuals interact socially can provide models for teaching; group investigation, jurisprudence, social inquiry, and laboratory learning are examples of how real-world situations can be replicated through teaching-learning activities (Joyce and Weil, 1972). Other examples are politics, community groups, legislative action, and business and industry (Gulley, 1960).

Any group can be addressed as either a single set or as subsets, and an educator can work with groups as units to enhance the learning potential through group processes and social constructs (Barker, 1987). Working with a group as a unit is possible because all groups have a psyche structure, and through this structure individuals deal with anxieties, doubts, and private desires. The group provides a structure for seeking comfort and reassurance; it is interactive; boundaries will emerge; and restrictions and demands on the group come from the task (Thelen, 1960).

The preceding chapters have presented a foundation for understanding the use and value of groups in teaching and learning. In this chapter, I will explore how the educator can construct activities to take advantage of the unique characteristics of the group. Management of a group is fundamental to its success, as nearly all the problems a group may encounter deal with a lack of understanding of group dynamics and how to manage the group process (Robson with Beary, 1995). As Cranton discussed in Chapter Three, the role of the educator will vary, depending on the type or function of the group.

Some adult educators interpret the concept of facilitator as becoming equal to the learners of the group. Although the adult educator is always a potential learner in the teaching-learning exchange, someone must be willing to bring to the group the ideas or issues the group may choose to avoid (Robson with Beary, 1995). At the least, the role of the adult educator with a group is to stimulate, organize, integrate, and otherwise bring to bear the potential of the group to deal with the task at hand (Wagner and Arnold, 1950). The adult educator's leadership of a group may include asking the initial questions, getting the group started and monitoring the process, and teaching group process skills. The educator is ultimately responsible for constructing the framework under which the group is to proceed with its learning task.

## Constructing Activities for Groups

Whether sculpting a process, illustrating an emotion, or applying multiple discussion techniques, little is done with groups that is truly new. Yet most of us can benefit from attempting to broaden our instructional range and using the group as the learning unit. Some general guidelines the adult educator can use in planning for group instruction include the following:

*Using the group: process versus content.* The *content* of an activity is made up of the topic and the substantive issues, the arguments advanced, and the words spoken about the topic during the activity. The *process* of the activity, however, refers to the nature of the relationships among the interacting individuals (Yalom, 1995). Bloom (1982) tells us that no matter how good the educator is in instructing the group, there will be great variations in the learning of the individuals in the group. Jarvis (1987) supports this notion by suggesting that one person's response to a situation may be totally different from another's. No situation has meaning in or for itself. What the group does is as strong a lesson for the participants as are the outcomes from discussion.

Experiences themselves do not teach without analysis or consideration. Processing following a discussion or activity allows for meaning to be constructed by the learner from the experience (Carlsen, 1988), and leading this processing is one of the adult educator's primary roles. The reflection that occurs during and after processing is very complex and involves both the cognitive and affective dimensions (Jarvis, 1987). Processing an activity or discussion is not just about what is said or done but also includes how, by whom, and when something was said or done, as well as what function the action or idea served in what group context (Miles, 1981).

*Incorporating the four C's: conflict, cooperation, challenge, content.* When constructing activities for groups, an educator uses the inherent motivators of conflict, cooperation, and challenge to create a situation and an activity for the participants. The role of the educator is to construct the activity so that some of each of the motivators are present; all three can be operationalized on several levels, independently or concomitantly. For example, is there conflict or cooperation or challenge within the individual, between the individual and the task, among the members of the group, between the group and the task, between the group or individual and the educator, or between the individual or group and the content? Conflict can result from something as simple as a missing piece of information or as complex as a hidden human dimension of another participant. Cooperation can be as minimal as each member of the group sharing a piece of information to the need to engage jointly in complex multilevel problem solving. Challenge refers often to the level of information and skill required to complete the assigned task and can be imposed by the educator constructing the activity with multiple dimensions of meaning.

As a concept in group activity construction, content is placed on a value level equal to these other concepts. In many situations, the same activity, be it game or discussion strategy, will work equally well for teaching different content. The processing and focus of the activity may vary, but the strategy remains constant. The social and affective outcomes desired as a result of that activity determine the specific strategy to use.

*Respecting differing learning styles.* By their nature, group activities appeal to different learning styles more than do lectures or information presentations. Yet educators must realize that not one group activity satisfies all learning styles; so they must construct activities with respect to the multiple learning styles and intelligences that exist. Whether the consideration is given to personality styles such as the Myers-Briggs Type Indicator or the Enneagram (see, for example Myers and McCaulley, 1987; Palmer, 1991), whole brain learning (Williams, 1983) or multiple intelligences (Gardner, 1993), incorporating different approaches within a strategy appeals to more learners more of the time. Within any activity, opportunities exist to appeal to individual learning preferences. For example, allowing for the silent generation of ideas prior to any discussion or activity satisfies one differing dimension of learners (Biehler and Snowman, 1986). A mini-lecture following a brainstorming activity or small-group discussion with reports back to the larger group can satisfy another dimension. Using an art-based activity and then requiring participants to interpret each other's images imposes a right brain–left brain relationship.

Activities must be constructed to engage learners in the kinds of thinking to be developed and to teach the specific cognitive operations needed to complete tasks successfully (Beyer, 1987). Whether learning is cooperative, collaborative, or transformative in nature, an activity is not successful if neither the critical thinking nor the requisite skills for the task are available to the learners. Activities must also be constructed so that they ultimately maintain the group focus, whether by open dialogue, by choral response to inquiry, or by individualized activity within the larger group process (Woolfolk, 1990). Varying types of group activities can address some differences within adult learning styles.

## Common Methods for Group Learning

Most adult educators have worked with groups using a variety of group processes. The more common techniques for group learning include discussion, gaming, role play, simulation, and projects.

*Discussion.* As noted in Chapter One, the discussion method has deep historical roots in American adult education, so it is not surprising that discussion is the basis for most group methods. Group discussion allows learners to express themselves clearly, to justify opinions, and to tolerate different views; it gives learners a chance to ask for clarification and obtain more information; and in discussion, learners assume responsibility by sharing the leadership of the group with the educator (Gilstrap and Martin, 1975). In addition to helping develop knowledge of content, discussion activities also develop leadership skills, summarize group opinion, move the group to consensus, require listening skills, permit learners to handle controversial topics, force participants to use paraphrasing skills, develop self-directed learning skills, and enhance the ability of participants to analyze, synthesize, and evaluate (Jacobsen, Eggen, and Kauchak, 1993).

The tasks of the educator in discussions are threefold: to ask questions that define the discussion or give it direction; to examine or query responses by drawing out reasons or implications; and to encourage dialogue when differing views exist (Adler, 1984). Kasulis (1984) views discussion as having three dimensions—the content, the process, and the persons—and suggests that the educator address all three in planning and facilitating the group.

A discussion may be structured many different ways, with each having a role in well-constructed educational programs. From the perspective of the educator, three broad purposes for discussion are intellectual, emotional, and social. For the participant, discussion techniques serve to address problem solving, issue or concept identification and exploration, consensus building, social and community building, and attitude change (Brookfield, 1990). Options for discussion available to the educator include brainstorming, participation training, fish bowl, Dear Ann-Andy, buzz group, rap group, Phillips 66, Samoan circle, forum, symposium, informal discussion group, panel discussion, Friends' meeting, listening teams, and appreciative inquiry. All of these techniques have been used with large and small groups and with a variety of topics and purposes. Information on these strategies is available in a wide array of texts on methods and group communications (for example, Abella, 1986; Nilson, 1993; Seaman and Fellenz, 1989).

Whatever the type of discussion, however, the facilitator has the responsibility for shaping the activity. Jacobsen, Eggen, and Kauchak (1993) identify five steps for the educator in using a discussion strategy: establishing the content, affect, and individual learner goals of the discussion; choosing the specific strategy for discussion most appropriate to those goals; constructing the discussion with cognizance of the learners' experience and knowledge; allocating time; and determining a specific product that will serve as an outcome from the activity such as a summary list, a series of conclusions, or a consensus.

*Gaming.* Another method often used in adult learning groups is gaming. Games in and of themselves are not educational; rather the context of the game creates learning opportunities to transfer affective awareness to a cognitive structure (Sutton-Smith, 1972). Games have rules and players (Cherfas, 1980) and share the elements of competition, chance, and reward. A challenge in gaming is the discrepancy that often exists between learning the strategies for the game and learning the concepts or relationships between concepts illustrated by the game (Novak, 1977). Ideas and inspiration for games for use in adult learning can emerge from childhood play, puzzles, riddles, board games, quiz shows, and a host of other sources such as books of games (see, for example, Fluegelman, 1976; Sutton-Smith, 1972). Games ultimately focus on psychological, social, or strategic outcomes.

*Role play.* Another common group method in adult education is role play, which is designed to allow participants and observers to experience how a given interaction may feel or look or sound. Following a simulation of a real or hypothetical situation, discussion and analysis occur focusing on how the interaction felt, what happened, and why (Abella, 1986).

Shaftel and Shaftel (1967) list nine steps of a classic role play: confronting the problem, selecting the role players, preparing the audience for participation as observers, setting the stage, enacting, discussing and evaluating, enacting further, discussing further, and sharing experiences and generalizing. Feedback from the observers is crucial to the success of a role play, because the intended outcome is understanding different ways of thinking or feeling.

*Simulation.* Another approach, often used in industry training, is to use simulations—events in which participants shape what happens within a constructed situation. Two assumptions of simulations are that (1) no structure of reality or human process that cannot be represented by a workable model exists, and (2) such a modeled experience promotes learning (Seaman and Fellenz, 1989). Another assumption about simulations is that a reality exists in the functions participants undertake, including what they say, do, and think. Two essential elements of a simulation are that (1) the event occurs in a simulated (that is not real) place—it is not the real world, so participants are able to make mistakes; and (2) the simulation requires a structure built around some problem or problems, and it must be sufficiently explicit to preserve the reality of function (Jones, 1982).

Although role plays and simulations are similar, two major distinctions exist between them. A role play includes an audience role, whereas a simulation involves all participants in the action; a role play focuses on the affective relationships, and a simulation focuses on an outcome.

*Projects.* A common group assignment is to develop a collective paper or report or similar project. Although projects often carry the baggage of negative prior experiences, in adult learning settings projects provide a quality of safety that is effective and helpful and that reflects the real world, as team projects are neither vicarious nor contrived (Vella, 1994). One successful technique for addressing the challenges of group projects is to require group projects to have, as a component of the effort, a presentation that must be creatively presented:

a skit, a piece of art work, or a process activity for the group. The presentation of the group project results is important, but time constraints often lead adult educators into the trap of setting expectations that result in nearly identical verbal reports. The guidelines presented by the educator will determine, to a great extent, the manner in which reports on projects or report-backs are presented.

*Other activities.* Almost any type of activity suitable for individual learning can be adapted to a group learning environment. Take, for example, the idea of drawing a picture to elicit an affective response to a topic. One group adaptation could be the development of pictures drawn by the small group, whereas another adaptation might be that individuals draw personal pictures but share major elements of their drawings with others in small groups and then receive feedback from the other participants. Construction blocks and toys make wonderful tools for small teams to use to construct models of abstract concepts or processes. Individual stream-of-consciousness journal writing after a group activity changes the dynamics of the journal writing process and can create a sense of collective action. Almost any individual educational activity can be adapted to a group, but it is important that the educator develop the activity with the concepts of process, skill, content, and outcome in mind.

## Tips for Group Activities

Any adult educator who has tried various group activities can attest to the value of experience. But many hard-learned rules of thumb do exist to help an educator move from limited activities to broader, more encompassing group teaching strategies—and to move with fewer pitfalls.

*Beware of bias for or against group activities.* Prior experience with groups will shape adults' views of group-based learning. Draves (1984) reminds us that some participants have had good experiences in groups, while others have not. Some individuals desire leadership roles, but others hope for minimal involvement. Clarity and authority on the part of the educator can minimize negative prior experiences. Expect participation rather than ask for it, and move quickly into an activity rather than wait until consensus is formed about participating. The latter usually allows too much time for learned patterns of social behavior to emerge. State the necessary information and rules for games or process for discussion, and have the groups immediately become involved. Far too many excellent activities are impaired when the educator tells the group in detail what will happen and what the outcome of the activity should be.

*Keep activities on track.* Part of the art of education is allowing for the unexpected—letting a group move in a direction it chooses. For some group purposes, though, such as problem solving or content mastery, this can be a setback. The major goal in discussion is to control and guide the process to ensure that it reaches some kind of conclusion or that issues become clearer (Highet, 1989). A simple tool for managing the tendency for a group to stray is to have the central topic, problem, issue, or task clearly defined and publicly placed for view on a chalkboard, flip chart, or poster.

*Ensure group participation.* One of the fears of many educators is that they will start an activity only to have the group rebel by not participating. A good rule of thumb for getting individuals involved and vocal is to focus on the affect and allow the cognitive components of the activity to emerge. Use the think-feel-believe rule: ask questions about what individuals think, feel, or believe, and there can be no wrong answers. This strategy also reduces the risk to the learners in participating.

*Be aware of speed and flow.* There is a rhythm to any group's behavior that is unique to that particular group of individuals. Attention to the rhythm of the group's behavior will maintain a smoothness and momentum in learning activities (Biehler and Snowman, 1986). Listen to a group—not to the words but to the tone of the group—and it is possible to hear the changes that occur when the group discovers something, or comes to consensus, or completes a task, or becomes redundant. Use the auditory but nonverbal component of the group to regulate the speed of the process.

*Establish group ground rules.* A time-honored tradition is using the group to establish its own rules for group membership and to enforce the group's norms. Using the group conscience to manage the behavior within the group works best in groups where individuals care about the opinions of their peers (Woolfolk, 1990). This suggests that one-time groups with less cohesion will be more likely to suffer from distractions and being off task than other types of groups. By placing and enforcing time constraints on activities, adult educators can help groups stay focused. Announce a time period for an activity that will force individuals to get on task quickly and remain so consistently.

*Create a climate for learning.* The environment for learning is more than the physical characteristics of the group and the room, yet the physical environment is centrally important (Bloom, 1982). The arrangement of chairs and tables, the placement of the facilitator, the lighting, the temperature, the colors, and even the clutter in a room can enhance or challenge group process and individual participation.

The affective environment the educator creates also has important ramifications (Heimlich and Norland, 1994). Does the group feel safe to discuss controversial topics? What is safe in terms of the affective environment to one learner may not be safe to another, however. A key for any educator is never to expect a group to do or reveal something the educator is not willing at that moment to do or reveal about himself or herself. Initially asking questions as discussed above and making certain that all comments are heard and appropriately supported ensures a relatively safe climate excluding issues of status and similar concerns within the group.

Participants in a group have both a primary task of being a member of the group and also secondary gratifications that can arise from interactions with the group. These secondary gratifications such as appearance to others, ego, attention needs, and so forth can severely undermine the effectiveness of a group activity (Yalom, 1995). A trick for a safe and effective means of addressing these secondary gratifications is to lay bare the process of the activity. Discuss with the group the functioning of the group. At most, individuals can self-disclose or at least self-discover their role in the group's interactions. This technique for addressing potentially harmful issues within the group has saved many activities and ensured a deeper understanding of both content and process in the groups involved.

*Make clear what will be learned from the activity.* Since the purpose of a learning group activity is education, it is important that the lessons be made explicit for the learners. Sometimes, the debriefing process can be open. Ask the participants, "What did you gain from this?" or, "Why do you think we did this activity?" In other situations, especially when time is a constraint, when the lessons may be embedded in the activity, or when the activity is too intense emotionally, the adult educator may need to provide a synthesis of the transferrable lessons of the group. One technique is to keep a flip chart record of underlying lessons as individuals share experiences, observations, or dialogue about the activity and then reveal these lessons with explanations and illustrations from the shared experiences.

There are numerous ways to develop activities, use activities, and process activities with groups. For each adult educator, however, what is most important is to experience the different ways of learning that are revealed when activities are varied, and the group develops fully its own personality, with the respect of the educator. As experience in facilitating group modes of learning is acquired, it becomes possible to use each group's distinctive process and personality as a guide for teaching strategies and activities. Effective group learning emerges from using the group as a learning unit and respecting both the psychological and sociological processes of the teaching-learning exchange.

**References**

Abella, K. T. *Building Successful Training Programs: A Step-by-Step Guide.* Reading, Mass.: Addison-Wesley, 1986.
Adler, M. J., and the Paideia Group. *The Paideia Program: An Educational Syllabus.* New York: Collier Books, 1984.
Barker, L. L. *Communication.* (4th ed.) Englewood Cliffs, N.J.: Prentice Hall, 1987.
Beyer, B. K. *Practical Strategies for the Teaching of Thinking.* Needham Heights, Mass.: Allyn & Bacon, 1987.
Biehler, R. F., and Snowman, J. *Psychology Applied to Teaching.* (5th ed.) Boston: Houghton Mifflin, 1986.
Bloom, B. S. *Human Characteristics and School Learning.* New York: McGraw-Hill, 1982.
Brookfield, S. D. *The Skillful Teacher: On Technique, Trust, and Responsiveness in the Classroom.* San Francisco: Jossey-Bass, 1990.
Carlsen, M. B. *Meaning-Making: Therapeutic Processes in Adult Development.* New York: Norton, 1988.
Cherfas, J. "It's Only a Game." In J. Cherfas and R. Lewin (eds.), *Not Work Alone: A Cross Cultural View of Activities Superfluous to Survival.* London: Temple Smith, 1980.
Draves, W. A. *How to Teach Adults.* Manhattan, Kans.: LERN, 1984.
Dworkin, M. S. *Dewey on Education.* New York: Teachers College Press, 1959.

Fluegelman, A. (ed.). *The New Games Book.* Garden City, N.Y.: Dolphin Books, 1976.
Gardner, H. *Multiple Intelligences: The Theory in Practice.* New York: HarperCollins, 1993.
Gilstrap, R. L., and Martin, W. R. *Current Strategies for Teachers: A Resource for Personalizing Education.* Pacific Palisades, Calif.: Goodyear, 1975.
Gulley, H. D. *Discussion, Conference, and Group Process.* Austin, Tex.: Holt, Rinehart and Winston, 1960.
Heimlich, J. E., and Norland, E. *Developing Teaching Style in Adult Education.* San Francisco: Jossey-Bass, 1994.
Highet, G. *The Art of Teaching.* New York: Vintage Books, 1989.
Jacobsen, D., Eggen, P., and Kauchak, D. *Methods for Teaching: A Skills Approach.* Columbus, Ohio: Merrill, 1993.
Jarvis, P. *Adult Learning in the Social Context.* London: Croom Helm, 1987.
Jones, K. *Simulations in Language Teaching.* New York: Cambridge University Press, 1982.
Joyce, B., and Weil, M. *Models of Teaching.* Englewood Cliffs, N.J.: Prentice Hall, 1972.
Kasulis, T. P. "Questioning." In M. M. Gullette (ed.), *The Art and Craft of Teaching.* Cambridge, Mass.: Harvard University Press, 1984.
Lawson, D. E. *Wisdom and Education.* Carbondale: Southern Illinois University Press, 1961.
Lovell, R. B. *Adult Learning.* London: Croom Helm, 1987.
Miles, M. B. *Learning to Work in Groups: A Practical Guide for Members and Trainers.* (2nd ed.) New York: Teachers College Press, 1981.
Myers, I. B., and McCaulley, M. H. *Manual: A Guide to the Development and Use of the Myers-Briggs Type Indicator.* Palo Alto, Calif.: Consulting Psychologists Press, 1987.
Nilson, C. *Team Games for Trainers.* New York: McGraw-Hill, 1993.
Novak, J. D. *A Theory of Education.* Ithaca, N.Y.: Cornell University Press, 1977.
Palmer, H. *The Enneagram: Understanding Yourself and the Others in Your Life.* San Francisco: HarperCollins, 1991.
Robson, M., with Beary, C. *Facilitating.* Brookfield, Vt.: Gower, 1995.
Seaman, D. F., and Fellenz, R. A. *Effective Strategies for Teaching Adults.* Columbus, Ohio: Merrill, 1989.
Shaftel, F. R., and Shaftel, G. *Role Playing for Social Values: Decision-Making in the Social Studies.* Englewood Cliffs, N.J.: Prentice Hall, 1967.
Sutton-Smith, B. *The Folkgames of Children.* Austin: University of Texas Press, 1972.
Thelen, H. A. *Education and the Human Quest.* New York: HarperCollins, 1960.
Vella, J. *Learning to Listen, Learning to Teach: The Power of Dialogue in Educating Adults.* San Francisco: Jossey-Bass, 1994.
Wagner, R. H., and Arnold, C. C. *Handbook of Group Discussion.* Boston: Houghton Mifflin, 1950.
Williams, L. V. *Teaching for the Two-Sided Mind: A Guide to Right Brain/Left Brain Education.* New York: Simon & Schuster, 1983.
Woolfolk, A. E. *Educational Psychology.* (4th ed.) Needham Heights, Mass.: Allyn & Bacon, 1990.
Yalom, I. D. *The Theory and Practice of Group Psychotherapy.* (4th ed.) New York: HarperCollins, 1995.


*JOE E. HEIMLICH is assistant professor of environmental education, School of Natural Resources, and leader, environmental science, OSU Extension, The Ohio State University, Columbus.*

*The concept of the "learning organization" is discussed, including the use of dialogue in group learning as a process for generative, creative, collective, and transformative learning.*

# Group Learning in the Workplace

G. Wayne West

Teamwork has become a major focus for many corporations as they seek to become more competitive and flexible. As baseball manager Casey Stengel once observed, "It's easy to get the players. Gettin' 'em to play together, that's the hardest part" (Clemmer, 1992, p. 193). In searching for how organizations can best "get their players to play together," companies are beginning to look inward. Rather than searching for outside gurus to provide solutions, organizations are tapping into learning and expertise that exist in-house among their own employees. Learning in the workplace has become a major portion of adult education, accounting for more than $52 billion ($210 billion by some estimates) per year in corporate expenditures (Watkins, 1995).

Workplace learning can refer to job-related instruction (training), to strategies for improving performance (human performance technology), to developing people as resources (human resource development), or to what learners do (Watkins, 1995). Workplace learning can also refer to individual learning, group learning, or organizational learning. Many companies are beginning to adopt the paradigm that learning is their business.

In this chapter, I will discuss how learning in the workplace has changed and what types of learning occur. The concept of the organization as a center of learning and the role of dialogue as a process for generative, creative, collective, and transformative learning will also be discussed. Group learning in the workplace, as characterized by the *learning organization* concept, represents an opportunity for adult educators to participate in the business and industry arena in a manner consistent with adult education principles.

## Changing Paradigms in the Workplace

Companies are discovering that "learning just in case" is not meeting the needs of a highly complex and rapidly changing environment. In the pre-industrial world, workers learned their craft on the job as apprentices to master craftsmen, a model that could be characterized as "learning just in time." With industrialization, rationality and efficiency became focal points, as evidenced by Taylor's scientific management approach. Work was divided into two categories: tasks performed by thinkers (management) and labor performed by nonthinkers (workers). The delivery system of learning in the workplace reflected the mechanistic structure of the organization, with trainers dispensing knowledge and workers being the passive recipients.

Embedded in this model are several commonly held assumptions of learning: everyone starts with the same base of knowledge; everyone learns at the same pace; listening is the best learning modality for all learners; everyone will bridge naturally from theory to application; individual learning is more desirable than collaborative learning; and learning is the transfer of knowledge from a teacher to a passive learner (Juechter, 1993).

The pressure for organizations to change comes from external sources such as the economic and political environments and from internal sources such as new technologies and the changing attitudes of members (Bouwen and Fry, 1991). The change seems to be from focusing on input (training and development) to output (performance). As organizations have adapted to meet the new challenges, the mechanistic method of learning has given way to an organic model that stresses horizontal communication, flexible structure, less hierarchical authority and control, and adaptability as compared to the highly vertical, inflexible structure of more traditional mechanistic models. Accompanying this change have been new assumptions regarding learning: learning is fundamentally social; knowledge is integrated into the life of communities; learning is an act of membership, not just the activity of a sole individual; knowing is engagement in practice; engagement is inseparable from empowerment; learning requires access and opportunity; and people are learning all of the time (Kahn, 1993).

**Types of Learning.** Much of the learning in the workplace has been adaptive. Individuals are trained to adapt to the needs of the organization in a manner that ensures consistency, integration, compliance with organizational norms, and maintenance of the status quo. The focus has been on controlling individuals rather than liberating them to be generative and productive. The new focus seems to be grappling with the realization that education is both controlling and liberating at the same time. The new paradigm encourages generative learning in order to bring forth people's ability to create.

David Sibbet of Graphics Guides, Inc., works with four levels of learning (Galagan, 1993): (1) learning to do work, (2) learning to do work more effectively, (3) learning to learn in the workplace, and (4) learning to reflect on the learning process itself. Levels 3 and 4 are the foci for those interested in learning becoming the business of organizations. The learning organization, as conceptualized by Senge (1990) or Watkins and Marsick (1993), builds on the double-loop learning concept of Argyris and Schön (1978). Learning to do work and to work more effectively are examples of adaptive learning. Learning to reflect on the learning process itself is reflective of the double-loop learning advocated by Argyris. Double-loop learning results in anticipative and generative learning, which enhances our ability to create rather than absorb knowledge (Senge, 1990). Table 6.1 illustrates some of the differences between the new paradigm of a learning organization and more traditional methods of learning, such as on-the-job training and the training classroom.

**Group Learning.** Learning in the workplace can be individual or group learning. The latter has received more attention, as organizations move from the mechanistic to the organic model. Much has been written about how to form teams, types of teams, what makes teams effective or ineffective, and leadership within teams, but little has been written about how teams learn (Dechant, Marsick, and Kasl, 1993). Attention has been on structure and product, not on process.

Group learning in the workplace is advocated for many reasons. Chief among them is that buy-in and ownership by workers in the process is increased by collaboration and inclusion. This becomes especially important when diversity exists within the workplace, including not only cultural, racial, and socioeconomic diversity but also diversity of thought (Folinsbee, 1995).

Table 6.1. Organizational Approaches to Learning

|  | Learning Organization | On-the-Job Training | Training Classroom |
|---|---|---|---|
| Leadership | Leadership is shared | Leader has expert knowledge and power | Trainer is authority |
| Type of learning | Generative | Adaptive | Anticipative |
| Knowledge production | Learners create knowledge | Others create knowledge | Others create knowledge |
| Power differentials | Learner is equal to others | Learner is dependent on master worker | Learner is dependent on trainer |
| Culture | Learning is valued | Performance is valued | Productivity is valued |
| Characteristics of the process | Facilitative | Sequential, rational | Seeks the one best way |
| Sequences | Experimenting, evaluating, questioning | Linear, step-by-step | Start and restart regression |

Traditional methods of coordination within organizations attempt to minimize diversity of thought and increase uniformity or conformity, but learning results from experimentation that crosses boundaries, and it may disrupt tried and true methods of the past.

## Learning Organizations

The learning organization as described by Senge (1990) consists of five disciplines—shared visions, mental models, personal mastery, team learning, and systems thinking—that are interrelated and interconnected. Organizations learn as a result of the individuals learning within them. Individuals who are committed to personal mastery strive to learn and form the basis for team learning to occur. Their mental models must be brought to the surface, then critically examined and shared in order for shared vision to occur. Shared vision comes from personal vision. The effort to narrow the gap between vision and reality leads individuals to strive for personal mastery. Systems thinking is the integration of the other disciplines with one another.

As discussed in Chapter Two, Dechant, Marsick, and Kasl (1993) have worked to construct a systems model of team learning. They draw from research on group processes, learning theory, and adult education research. The model provides a theoretical framework of how team learning takes place in the learning organization and proposes four developmental stages of learning that are progressive, although Kasl, Dechant, and Marsick (1993) do not disallow the possibility of regression. The group moves from all learning taking place within the individual (contained learning) to a phase in which learners share information and meaning perspectives but have not yet experienced having knowledge that is uniquely the group's own (collected learning). Following the collected learning phase, members of the group begin to integrate their knowledge and meaning perspectives, allowing for the creation of knowledge by the group (constructed learning). The final phase is one of a habitual process of transformation of experience into group knowledge (continuous learning).

In addition to proposing the developmental phases of group learning, Kasl, Dechant, and Marsick (1993) have constructed a systems model of inputs (team learning conditions and organizational learning conditions) to the learning process and outputs (team learning outcomes and organizational learning contributions). Learning follows four processes—framing and reframing, integrating perspectives, experimenting, and crossing boundaries—that revolve around collective thinking and action by the group. Their work allows us to look at how group learning begins and develops in the learning organization.

**Transformative Learning.** The goal of organizational learning is to transform the organization, which is a somewhat different goal for transformative learning than that discussed in Chapter Three. Continuous learning by all members within the organization is stressed by those interested in transformation. Traditional learning in the organization reacts to external or internal problems. A major task of any organization wanting to transform itself is to reflect critically on current assumptions. Reactive learning is the enemy of continuous learning (Kofman and Senge, 1993) because it leads to a philosophy of "if it isn't broken, don't fix it" and inhibits experimentation and learning that could lead to the improvement of products or processes. It also seems to lead to the belief that if it is broken, an expert is needed to fix it. Rarely in the traditional model are employees viewed as the best consultants available (Clemmer, 1992).

One of the tasks of those interested in transformative learning is to shift organizational meaning perspectives, which are a composite of "specific knowledge, beliefs, value judgments, and feelings that constitute interpretations of experience" (Mezirow, 1991, pp. 5–6). Most groups have a task-oriented meaning perspective that results in interaction being task achievement. If the meaning perspective can be shifted to learning, the goal becomes generative learning (Kasl, Dechant, and Marsick, 1993).

The importance of reflecting critically on our assumptions is highlighted by the gap that exists between what we say we believe and what we do. Argyris and Schön (1978) refer to this difference as espoused theories versus theories-in-use. Organizations develop theories of action also, and they too experience the gap between espoused theories and theories-in-use. These theories result from the need to remain in control, maximize winning and minimize losing, suppress negative feelings, and be as rational as possible (Argyris, 1991).

Reality is based on the assumptions we make. Isaacs (1993) talks of how humans perceive the world and then take action based on those perceptions. We divide the world into categories of thought and make distinctions between those categories—but then forget that we have created the categories and act as if they represent an absolute reality. Organizations have also been constructed into categories, on the basis of assumptions that we treat as if they were perfectly representative of reality.

These perceptions lead to competition and defensiveness by the parts of an organization rather than cooperation and movement by the whole. Competition, fragmentation, and reactiveness are the main dysfunctional behaviors in organizations (Kofman and Senge, 1993). As members become more specialized in their knowledge, they become more isolated from one another. Rather than learning from one another and valuing differences, they tend to compete and defend a point of view or position. What is needed is an effort to reason together, not defend turf.

**Barriers to Learning.** Defensive routines prevent learning. Over the fifteen years he has been studying management consultants, Argyris (1991) has found that, when the quest for continuous improvement turns to internal factors rather than external factors, defensive routines appear. Why do professionals become so defensive when they examine their own behavior? Embarrassment leads to what Schein (1993) refers to as mutual face saving. As a method of saving face, individuals engage in societal niceties that may aid social relations but harm communication, understanding, and learning. In reality, the main purpose behind defensive routines is not to preserve social relations but to hide our reasoning behind our views.

Defensive routines are provoked by the suggestion that we create our own realities through our actions. If we accept this premise, then we also accept that our problems arise from our own policies, decisions, strategies, and action. Behaviors that act as defensive routines are to smooth things over and avoid talking about the real issues, or the opposite—to speak out in a no-holds-barred manner or to engage in a winner-take-all, free-for-all opinion battle (Senge, 1990). The objective of defensive routines is to minimize threat and embarrassment to ourselves. Saving face becomes of paramount importance.

In part, this occurs because of the way professionals view failure. Most professionals do not see failure as necessary to learning. In fact, few have had opportunities to learn from failure since they tend to be successful at what they do (Argyris, 1991). While this makes them very good at single-loop learning (focusing on external factors), it interferes with and prevents double-loop learning (focusing on internal factors). It leads to a fear of failure and a view that to fail is both shameful and deplorable. If they are not recognized by others as successful, professionals go into what Argyris calls the "doom loop of despair."

**Dialogue as a Means of Learning.** Team learning becomes a method of dealing with defensive routines by allowing them to surface through self-disclosure and inquiry by means of dialogue. Dialogue is seen as an essential component of team learning by Senge (1990), Argyris and Schön (1978), Isaacs (1993), and Schein (1993). It allows a group to think generatively, creatively, and together (Schein, 1993). The goal of dialogue is to help the group bring assumptions to the surface and clarify theories-in-use, which must happen before a shared set of meanings and a common thinking process can be developed.

Emphasizing shared concepts or mental models does not imply that everyone thinks alike. Groupthink—when people succumb to group pressure for conformity—is not a desirable condition. Group intelligence, where people reason and think collectively, is (Senge, 1990).

Dialogue is a discipline of collective thinking and inquiry. The process allows for transforming the thinking that lies behind the words that are said (Isaacs, 1993). Underlying assumptions that compose our behavior, thoughts, and experiences can be explored in a manner that allows individuals to step outside their position and observe their own conversation and thought process.

Dialogue is neither discussion nor debate. The term *dialogue* stems from the Greek words *dia*, meaning flowing through, and *logos*, meaning word or speech (Senge, 1990). Discussion means to break apart, and debate means to beat down (Isaacs, 1993). When we discuss or debate, we are trying to score points or to win a person over to our position. But in dialogue, there is a suspension of our assumptions and a willingness to openly examine all possibilities.

The evolution of dialogue proposed by Isaacs (1993) clarifies how dialogue and discussion or debate follow different tracks. Isaacs charts out how conversations occur in "containers" that are fields of genuine meeting and inquiry. What begins as conversation is influenced by crisis of suspension and crisis of collective pain leading to either dialogue or discussion. Dialogue can lead to metalogue—moving with or among the group—whereas discussion can lead to debate—the beating down of opposing ideas.

The instability of the container results from the individual differences people bring to the group and the conflict and defensive routines that result. When people engage in conversation, they begin the process of coming together and sharing. Sharing diverse ideas leads to a weighing out or deliberation process. At this point, an individual decides whether to suspend assumptions and move toward dialogue or to move on to greater instability. People will move back and forth between suspending assumptions and analyzing or discussing. As this vacillation occurs, the group will become uncomfortable as the positions become more polarized and defended, but this process helps to bring hidden differences to the surface. If the group can explore these differences and keep listening in order to learn, the crisis of suspension will be managed. The focus of the group can become collective inquiry, with new insights being developed. Members begin to understand how isolation and fragmentation are created through their own assumptions. The crisis of collective pain refers to the challenge of accepting self-created limits. As a group navigates this crisis, it moves into a phase in which "information in the process contains as much meaning as the content of the words exchanged" (Isaacs, 1993, p. 38).

Discussion and debate can be valid problem-solving and decision-making processes if all group members understand one another enough to speak the same language (Schein, 1993). In today's high-velocity environments, however, organizations more often than not are fragmented, and their members are not even speaking to each other. Senge (1990) discusses the need for alignment within groups for team learning to occur. A group is aligned when it functions as a whole, as opposed to working at cross-purposes. When people work collectively toward the same ends, a synergy develops.

Dialogue allows for the transformation of organizations, with members moving from individual, competing parts that are walled off from one another and reacting to external factors, to a collective, generative, boundary-crossing group engaged in double-loop learning. Just as Mezirow (1991) discusses the role of dialogue in reflecting critically on uncritically accepted meaning perspective for individuals, groups can do the same together.

**Capturing Learning.** It is important to capture group learning so that it can become part of a knowledge repository. Unless companies create knowledge repositories that employees can access easily and openly, they are doomed to participate in "the Santayana Review," which is based on George Santayana's words, "Those who cannot remember the past are condemned to repeat it" (Garvin, 1994, p. 24). Knowledge repositories can also aid the transfer of learning across boundaries.

Memory and learning are intertwined so that they influence one another. Learning is the acquisition of knowledge, and memory is the retention of knowledge (Kim, 1993). But memory is not considered to be simply a storage device that permits the recall of trivia in order to win a game. Memory is an active component of learning, as in Senge's mental models. Mental models represent a worldview, and when they are shared, they represent the team's worldview. As Senge says, "Mental models are active—they shape how we act (1990, p. 175)." If the learning of individuals is not transferred to the group, or from the group to the organization, the learning will be lost. Institutional memory allows for new learning to build on past learning.

Organizations with 40 to 50 percent turnover experience severe problems with learning because the knowledge base is eroded (Kim, 1993) and maintaining the shared mental models that allow for group learning is difficult. Learning without change occurs when there is no transfer from the individual to the team or when teams fail to share their learning across time or across vertical, horizontal, external, and geographic boundaries (Ulrich, Von Glinow, and Jick, 1993). Garvin (1994) suggests reports, tours, cross-training, personnel rotation plans, and training as methods for transferring learning. By sharing learning across boundaries, it becomes less person-dependent and more embedded in the systems of the organization (Watkins and Marsick, 1993). Electronic networks offer promise as repositories of knowledge. They can become the libraries of learning for organizations (Senge, 1990).

## Conclusion

To deal with the continuous nature of change, learning in the workplace will remain a major focus of adult educators. Dialogue will continue to be an important component of group learning, as corporations embrace greater diversity and place greater emphasis on the creation of knowledge by workers. Learning is the result of interacting with the environment and with coworkers. If we are to produce knowledge as workers, we will move toward rewarding cooperation and collaboration rather than competition between individuals. Alignment, shared mental models, and constant reflection on underlying assumptions will be major foci of group learning in the workplace. The emphasis will shift from training to learning.

The world of work is changing, and the way we conceptualize work will change. Instead of learning jobs, we must begin to learn about working under different conditions. The prospect of doing the same job for thirty years is dimming. In its place is the concept of working in multiple roles and on multiple teams. Greater emphasis will be placed on learning processes and on how groups work. Interpersonal relations, communication skills, self-analysis, and reflection will receive greater attention. A great need exists for further research leading to a theory of group learning.

In Chapter Seven, Brad Cahoon writes about the role of technology in group learning. Clearly, we can anticipate the increasing use of the Internet and the World Wide Web as tools for workplace learning by groups. In addition, computers will be used for what Senge (1990, p. 406) refers to as "microworlds," to allow employees to learn from experimentation. Microworlds are designed microcosms of reality that can be conducted as computerized simulations. The advantage of microworlds is that participants can get firsthand experience without risking their own or the corporation's well-being. By compressing time and space, microworlds allow us to go into the future and learn what happens as a result of our decisions.

The changing paradigm in the workplace has created an environment that emphasizes learning as the core activity of businesses. The need for quick responses to change and complexity challenges bureaucratic structures that are rigid and slow to react. The learning organization, with its emphasis on personal mastery, team learning, and the use of technology to allow learning to be tested may be the model of the future for organizations that champion generative learning over adaptive learning. Dialogue is the central process within the learning organization that allows transformative learning to occur. Certainly, the optimism and excitement present in the literature warrant a critical review of the concept.

Some cautionary notes are being sounded about the move toward learning organizations. Kerka (1995) cites several examples of organizations that have implemented learning organization concepts with less than desirable results. Jacobs (1995) and West (1994) cite a lack of critical analysis regarding learning organizations. Perhaps more alarming is the charge that management approaches framed in "the language of worker participation and quality are newer and more sophisticated ways to control workers" (Schied, 1996, p. 62). Group learning in the workplace is fertile ground for research, not only to find out how it occurs but to discover for whose purpose and whose benefit it occurs.

## References

Argyris, C. "Teaching Smart People How to Learn." *Harvard Business Review,* 1991, 69 (3), 99–109.

Argyris, C., and Schön, D. A. *Organizational Learning: A Theory of Action Perspective.* San Francisco: Jossey Bass, 1978.

Bouwen, R., and Fry, R. "Organizational Innovation and Learning: Four Patterns of Dialog Between the Dominant Logic." *International Studies of Management and Organizations,* 1991, 21 (4), 37–51.

Clemmer, J. *Firing on All Cylinders: The Service/Quality System for High-Powered Corporate Performance.* Homewood, Ill.: Business One Irwin, 1992.

Dechant, K., Marsick, V., and Kasl, E. "Towards a Model of Team Learning." *Studies in Continuing Education,* 1993, 15 (1), 1–14.

Folinsbee, S. W. "Workplace Basics in the 1990s: Critical Issues and Promising Practices." In W. F. Spikes (ed.), *Workplace Learning.* New Directions for Adult and Continuing Education, no. 68. San Francisco: Jossey Bass, 1995.

Galagan, P. A. "Helping Groups Learn." *Training and Development,* 1993, 47, 57–61.

Garvin, D. A. "Building a Learning Organization." *Business Credit,* 1994, 96, 19–28.

Isaacs, W. N. "Taking Flight: Dialogue, Collective Thinking, and Organizational Learning." *Organizational Dynamics,* 1993, 22 (2), 24–39.

Jacobs, R. L. "Impressions About the Learning Organization." *Human Resource Development Quarterly,* 1995, 6 (2), 119–122.

Juechter, W. M. "Learning by Doing." *Training and Development,* 1993, 47, 29–30.
Kahn, T. M. *A New Learning Agenda: Putting People First.* Palo Alto, Calif.: Institute for Research on Learning, 1993.
Kasl, E., Dechant, K., and Marsick, V. "Living the Learning: Internalizing Our Model of Group Learning." In D. Boud, R. Cohen, and D. Walker (eds.), *Using Experience for Learning.* Bristol, Pa.: Society for Research into Higher Education and Open University Press, 1993.
Kerka, S. *The Learning Organization: Myths and Realities.* Columbus: ERIC Clearinghouse on Adult, Career, and Vocational Education, Center on Education and Training for Employment, Ohio State University, 1995.
Kim, D. H. "The Link Between Individual and Organizational Learning." *Sloan Management Review,* 1993, 35, 37–50.
Kofman, F., and Senge, P. M. "Communities of Commitment: The Heart of the Learning Organizations." *Organizational Dynamics,* 1993, 22 (2), 4–23.
Mezirow, J. *Transformative Dimensions of Adult Learning.* San Francisco: Jossey-Bass, 1991.
Schein, E. H. "On Dialogue, Culture, and Organizational Learning." *Organizational Dynamics,* 1993, 22 (2), 40–51.
Schied, F. M. "Organizational Learning and Control: A Critical Examination of HRD and the Politics of Workplace Discipline." In P. Cunningham, W. Lawrence, and W. Miranda (eds.), *Selected Papers from the Fifth Annual LEPs Research Symposium: Critical Perspectives.* DeKalb: Northern Illinois University, 1996.
Senge, P. M. *The Fifth Discipline.* New York: Currency Doubleday, 1990.
Ulrich, D., Von Glinow, M. A., and Jick, T. "High Impact Learning: Building and Diffusing Learning Capability." *Organizational Dynamics,* 1993, 22 (2), 52–66.
Watkins, K. "Workplace Learning: Changing Times, Changing Practices." In W. F. Spikes (ed.), *Workplace Learning.* New Directions for Adult and Continuing Education, no. 68. San Francisco: Jossey-Bass, 1995.
Watkins, K. E., and Marsick, V. J. *Sculpting the Learning Organization: Lessons in the Art and Science of Systemic Change.* San Francisco: Jossey Bass, 1993.
West, G. W. "Learning Organizations: A Critical Review." In L. Martin (ed.), *Proceedings of the Thirteenth Midwest Research-to-Practice Conference.* Milwaukee: University of Wisconsin-Milwaukee, 1994.

*G. WAYNE WEST is a doctoral candidate studying adult education and organizational change at The Ohio State University.*

*Technology in group learning is discussed; examples of Internet-based instruction illustrate how distributed computing can situate and engage groups of learners.*

# Group Learning and Technology

*Brad Cahoon*

Since the introduction of personal computers in the early 1980s, millions of office workers have adapted to the daily use of complex hardware and software. In most organizations, computer users cope with their constantly changing tools with limited training (Bikson, 1987; Olsten Forum for Information Management, 1993). Although the term *personal computer* suggests individual, isolated users, in fact information technology tends to promote group learning, as work group members share the challenges of solving computer problems, giving and receiving informal instruction, and negotiating new workplace roles (Cahoon, 1995). Local area networks and the Internet have accelerated demands for new technological skills, uniting novices and experts in a need for continuous learning (Brown and Duguid, 1992) and offering new resources to make this learning possible.

Encounters with information technology in educational settings tend to be more structured and less driven by innovation than the improvisational, just-in-time learning of work groups. In spite of often-echoed calls from instructional technologists for paradigm shifts and learner empowerment, most schools still use technology primarily to augment teacher-led instruction or to support self-directed learning. For now, the unique relationship between technological change and group learning is more apparent outside the academy than within it.

In this chapter, I will suggest alternative roles for technology in group educational activities, based on studies of computer skill learning in the workplace and other research about how work groups learn and share technological skills. I will interpret this research in the context of theories of situated learning and discuss some creative examples of technology-based education.

## Distributed Computing: Terminology and Background

In this chapter, the term *technology* is used synonymously with *information technology*—electronic tools for communication. Such tools are usually categorized as *synchronous* or *asynchronous* (McGrath and Hollingshead, 1994). Users of synchronous technologies like the telephone, video teleconferencing, and Internet Relay Chat (IRC) send and receive messages in a continual exchange. Print, voice mail, videotape, and e-mail are asynchronous, allowing users to deliver and respond to messages at any time and in any order.

Synchronous technologies have received greater attention in educational research, perhaps because they are more readily adapted to the familiar classroom model in which teachers and students meet at specified times for lectures, discussion, and assessment. In such a model, technology is primarily a transmission medium; ideally, it is transparent to learners and irrelevant to the content of instruction. However, this adaptation of information technologies to the culture of traditional schooling bears little resemblance to the ways in which adults learn technological skills in the workplace. There, far from being transparent, computers and networks demand attention for both their complexities and their power to enhance performance. This chapter will focus on some asynchronous technologies enabled by networked personal computers, particularly electronic mailing lists and the World Wide Web.

Skill with computer applications like word processors and spreadsheets has become a basic job requirement for most office work. The business value of software applications is enhanced by local area networks (LANs) that connect computers to each other and to storage systems (file servers). By allowing users to share computer-generated documents (files), networks enable new forms of group work. As Crook (1994) observes, "Files become objects that a community of users may view, share and transform . . . much as they might manipulate resources in the material (non-computed) world" (p. 195). The widespread adoption of software standards for the interconnection of networks has produced the Internet, a global medium for communication and access to shared data. The World Wide Web, which allows the creation and distribution of hypertext documents containing images, audio, and video, is a recent and highly visible example of the evolution of the Internet (Berners-Lee, 1996).

Both within organizations and between them, electronic mail (the asynchronous transmission of text messages) has become a pervasive tool. Like the telephone, its simplicity allows it to be adapted to many purposes. As the Internet has spawned geographically dispersed communities of researchers, hobbyists, and others with shared interests, e-mail has evolved to support group learning and other forms of collaboration through the creation of mailing lists, Usenet news groups, and web-based conferencing systems. Mailing lists support a simple conferencing model suitable for relatively small groups, in which messages are sent to an automated mail system (often called a *listserv*) for redistribution to an entire group of subscribers. This relatively primitive technology is used for discussion, research, and education in a wide range of subject areas.

Recently, text-based conferencing capabilities have been incorporated into the World Wide Web, allowing participants to read and contribute to discussions through the same browser software they use for viewing hypertext documents (Woolley, 1996). By offering a single user interface to diverse network resources, the World Wide Web removes many of the special skill requirements for asynchronous collaboration and learning.

In the second half of the 1990s, business networks are expanding and connecting to the Internet, leading to astonishingly rapid growth in the size and activity of the global network. Basic tools of distributed computing—applications, e-mail, and the World Wide Web—are becoming almost as pervasive as the telephone and television in countries with well-developed information infrastructures. As the technological resources of businesses and educational institutions become more similar and as educational institutions face increasing pressure to adapt to these technologies, it may be useful to examine how work groups learn with and about technology and to analyze some formal and informal educational programs that rely on similar modes of learning.

## Computer Skill Learning in the Workplace

Surprisingly little is known about the processes through which adults develop computer skills. Understanding these processes may be critical to the resolution of the so-called productivity paradox. This phenomenon is the disparity between the huge investments organizations have made in information technology during the past few decades and the flat growth of productivity over the same period (Landauer, 1995). The productivity paradox is the result of many factors, but one of the most important may be a lack of effective training and education. The proliferation of computer training workshops and evening classes, books, videotapes, television programs, and computer-assisted tutorials reflects both the scope of this educational need and the inadequacy of organizational efforts to address it.

The characteristics of the motor, perceptual, and cognitive skills underlying computer use are better understood than the processes of their acquisition (see Card, Moran, and Newell, 1983; Gattiker, 1992; Waern, 1989). Some studies (Carroll, 1990; Czaja, Hammond, Blascovich, and Swede, 1986; Czaja, Hammond, Blascovich, and Swede, 1989; Gist, Rosen, and Schwoerer, 1988; Gist, Schwoerer, and Rosen, 1989) suggest that classroom instruction and self-directed tutorials are relatively inefficient in developing transferable computer skills. One comparative case study indicates that informal group learning plays a more important role in computer skill learning than formal training (Cahoon, 1995).

In this study, interviews with work groups in three organizations—departments within a university, a hospital, and a publishing firm—revealed patterns of behavior consistent with other studies of work group computing (such as Bullen and Bennett, 1991) and situated learning (Hutchins, 1995; Lave and Wenger, 1991). The participants reported that informal interactions with other members of their work groups were more instrumental in their skill development than participation in training. Typically, these interactions involved identifying local experts, one-on-one tutoring, solving problems together, and deciding who would do what computer tasks.

All the participants named other work group members to whom they turned routinely for computer help. Some knowledge critical to job performance could be communicated to novices only by such local experts. For example, new employees needed familiarity with file names and the organization of directories to perform even the most basic tasks, regardless of previous computer experience.

One-to-one tutoring by a local expert was a particularly valuable but time-intensive activity that usually occurred only when a new member joined a work group or when tasks were reassigned. A typical tutoring episode involved a local expert and a trainee working together at the same computer the trainee was to use for the task.

Local experts were not the sole sources of computer information. Potentially, every member of the work group was a learning resource for all the others. Asking and answering questions was reported to be the most common method of solving computer problems. Sometimes questions were perceived as inappropriate because of their time costs to other members of the work group; however, not asking a question could be equally expensive.

Either explicitly or implicitly, the members of the work groups negotiated informal rules for managing the distribution of computer knowledge and work. These rules varied, depending on the weight each work group gave to differences in status and authority. Some groups granted local experts considerable authority to encourage or coerce colleagues to take responsibility for their own computer skill development. In other groups, supervisors and professionals delegated almost all computer work to clerical staff who lacked the political or cultural leverage to change the distribution of knowledge, with the result that little group learning occurred.

Interpersonal behaviors like solving problems together and deciding who would do which tasks all arose naturally from the shared goals and constraints of the work groups as they used available computer resources to perform their jobs. In addition to hardware and software skills, this learning involved the acceptance of social roles, attitudes, and expectations that framed the learners' understandings of computer work.

The theory of legitimate peripheral participation advanced by Lave and Wenger (1991) helps to explain such situated learning. Typical of many work groups, legitimate peripheral participation is a process by which newcomers are integrated into the productive activities of a group. On-the-job learning through observation of and tutoring by old-timers is legitimized by the culture of the organization. Novices are assigned peripheral positions and tasks that allow them to see complex work being done. Over time, novices become full participants. Their acceptance as peers doing equal work is a process of socialization in which they accept the goals and practices of the group, including the responsibility to help educate future novices.

Two points about computer skill learning in work groups are particularly relevant to other group learning situations. First, the development of practical computer skills is usually part of a broader process of socialization. Skills are developed through observation of and interaction with more experienced members of the work group, and increased knowledge is marked by changes in social roles. Cognitive changes are situated in a context of social action (Brown, Collins, and Duguid, 1988). Second, ad hoc coaching from other work group members, often prompted by an immediate work need, seems to transfer more strongly to practice than formal training. Coaching in the workplace on the same computer the learner would later use for the task was generally perceived as more efficient than training conducted in another setting (a finding consistent with the experimental results of Singley and Anderson, 1989).

## Distributed Computing for Group Learning: Two Examples

Not all the circumstances that support informal learning in work groups can be reproduced in formal training or education. Work group membership tends to be stable over longer periods of time. The shared goals, constraints, and resources of work over an extended period provide a basis for stronger relationships and individual identification with the group, which in turn motivate learning and teaching. Economic incentives and the perceived importance of labor have a motivational force often absent in school, where the purposes and consequences of action are more abstract and where the participants' previous educational experiences tend to reinforce attitudes of passivity and dependency. Nonetheless, the use of distributed computing can infuse educational activities with some of the group dynamics typical of the workplace.

Increasingly, innovative educators are developing courses and programs that use technology to engage students with knowledge and with one another in new ways. At the same time, the virtual communities enabled by the Internet are creating their own systems for teaching and learning that bypass institutional education altogether. Out of many possible examples, I chose two to examine in this chapter: a George Mason University seminar taught primarily via the World Wide Web and a mailing list that unites software developers, expert users, and novices in a dynamic learning community.

**Taming the Electronic Frontier.** A faculty member at George Mason University (GMU), Brad Cox, uses both synchronous and asynchronous technologies to teach "Taming the Electronic Frontier," a core course in computer-based communication for a master's in telecommunications program (Cox, 1996). Originally conceived as a conventional seminar, Cox was inspired by the needs of the program's nontraditional students to move to a technology-based format that allows more flexibility and independence. After the first night, class attendance is optional. Cox teaches from the GMU television studio, and lectures are available via local cable TV or videotape. However, he claims, "television is the least important and most expendable and problematic part of our infrastructure," primarily because it limits group interactions. Cox's solution has been to take advantage of the Internet's ability to create "experiential learning communities."

Students work and interact primarily through the course's web site (accessible from http://www.virtualschool.edu/). Cox's web pages for each week of the course provide announcements, syllabus information, and task assignments, all of which require participants to use computers. They may work at their homes, offices, or the GMU computer labs, submitting homework via World Wide Web forms, news groups, e-mail, and their own web pages. Cox publishes all student assignments on the web site: "Since the task results are public information, this creates an additional learning channel through which those having problems can learn from those who've completed the tasks successfully" (Cox, 1996).

The technological challenges of such a course are obvious. Finding computing resources, getting computer novices connected, and building the basic skills necessary to participate in the on-line course might have seemed insurmountable obstacles to many teachers. Cox has overcome these problems by relying on the students' willingness to assist one another. Using the telephone, e-mail, and the course's news group, students describe their problems and help each other find solutions. Additionally, Cox assigns team projects designed to make the course more accessible and powerful each time it is offered. For 30 percent of their grade, teams are instructed to "pick any breakdown that has annoyed you this semester" and "eliminate it." Outcomes have ranged from student-developed tutorials to major changes in GMU's Internet policies and resources. These projects initially brought Cox and his students into conflict with university administrators reluctant to support changes, but class meetings with administrators led to a more supportive, "customer-oriented attitude that views student initiatives as the solution, not the problem."

A software engineer, Cox sees the student-driven evolution of "Taming the Electronic Frontier" as analogous to the iterative process by which customers and developers refine software through ongoing analysis and revision. A top-down instructional design that attempted to specify all aspects of the course in advance could not have produced the remarkable student contributions that continue to improve the course. Cox is well aware, however, that "any shift in power from teachers toward students implies tension over differing ideas of quality." He cites as an example an assignment in which students build a web-based "product": "Grades for this task are assigned by 'selling' the products in an electronic market for peer assessment. I find it intriguing, but troubling, that students often assign high value to products that emphasize flash and glitter at the expense of academic substance . . . this is a clear caution that a careful balance of power between teacher and student is necessary instead of either extreme."

**Frontier-Talk.** Brad Cox's course demonstrates how distributed computing can enable new forms of group learning within traditional academic instruction, but for many years, users of the Internet have spontaneously created similar learning communities through mailing lists and news groups. The

Frontier-Talk mailing list is by no means unique, but it provides a representative example of how on-line communities coalesce around common educational needs and create impressive instructional resources with little centralized planning or design.

Like most successful mailing lists, Frontier-Talk is deliberately narrow in scope. Its participants are the developers and users of a free Macintosh software tool, Frontier, created and distributed by Dave Winer (Winer, 1996). Frontier provides a scripting language and database system that allow users to automate common Macintosh tasks and to control other programs. In May 1996, about 550 people were receiving daily e-mail from Frontier-Talk. Frontier's noncommercial status means that all technical support and instruction are provided by the community of users. The ways the members of Frontier-Talk have responded to this situation often parallel the ways in which work groups share computer skills.

Most of the learning activities of the mailing list members appear to be directly related to work projects—for example, configuring a World Wide Web server or automating tasks for newspaper production. Unlike most academic learning activities, in which the transfer of knowledge to practical tasks is anticipated but rarely tested, the daily commerce of Frontier-Talk consists of questions and answers about technical tasks, with immediate consequences for the participants. While the members of the mailing list appear to represent a wide range of professions and activities (including electronic and print publishing, programming, consulting, research, and higher education), this shared concern with problem solving creates a sense of common purpose in which individual crises receive immediate group support and successful "hacks" are mutually celebrated.

Another similarity to work group learning is the role of local experts. The most experienced users of Frontier (including its creator) regularly respond to novice questions, explaining features of the software and providing solutions to specific problems. As in work groups, the members of Frontier-Talk negotiate explicit and implicit rules for managing the time costs of novice learning needs. In their responses to questions, experts often refer participants to available on-line documentation, including searchable archives of past messages to the mailing list. Participants asking basic questions without consulting these resources are sometimes criticized but rarely ignored.

Some expert list members have voluntarily created web-based tutorials and instruction manuals to address novice learning needs, often incorporating text from discussions on the mailing list. These instructional tools are publicized, critiqued, and revised through discussion on the list. In many cases, these tutorials document the results of self-directed learning, recorded so that other members of the group can recapitulate it. Sharing these solutions is encouraged by the culture of Frontier-Talk and provides a means for novices (*newbies*) to assume new roles as experts (*gurus*).

As in other technology-oriented communities, these status demarcations are flexible and serve more to channel questions appropriately than to consolidate the authority of individuals. Rapid change ensures that experts must learn continually to maintain their status, a phenomenon noted by Brown and Duguid (1992) in computer user groups: "Given the rapidly changing technology, the user groups implicitly understand that, at some time and in some way, anyone can be both a novice and an expert" (p. 173).

Far from being unusual, Frontier-Talk is typical of the ways in which Internet communities identify and reinforce expertise, solve problems collaboratively, and provide instruction for newcomers.

## Conclusion

The World Wide Web and other manifestations of distributed computing have been hailed widely as marking the advent of a new era for education. "Taming the Electronic Frontier" and Frontier-Talk are early realizations of this potential. However, a wide gap still separates the learning cultures associated with technology and its users from those of academia.

Groups learning about computers and networks "in the wild" (Hutchins, 1995) use their information technologies as media that can both store and enact the concepts and procedures needed to perform tasks. In these work environments, knowledge and skills are distributed in ways that complicate the observation and assessment of learning immensely, since the cognitive processes of individuals cannot be separated from the logic and information embedded in their technology or from the processes of informal instruction and socialization occurring within the group. Such groups rely almost completely on actual work tasks to structure their members' learning, as opposed to formal training or education.

The studies indicating that computer training does not always transfer efficiently to work practices should serve as a warning about academic activities that attempt to transpose familiar classroom methods to technology-based instruction, whether in video classrooms and computer labs or on the Internet. The ways in which work groups rely on just-in-time interactions with local experts, whether within a shared office or through an exchange of Internet e-mail, call into question many deeply ingrained assumptions about the role of instructors and the deferred use of knowledge. Rather than attempting to adapt technology to the culture of traditional schooling, educators should consider how tools like e-mail, on-line conferencing, and the World Wide Web stimulate new patterns of interaction and how their teaching methods can be adapted to forms of group learning that are spontaneous, uncredentialed, and increasingly pervasive.

## References

Berners-Lee, T. "A General Overview of the World Wide Web." [http://www.w3.org/pub/WWW/Talks/General.html]. Apr. 1996.

Bikson, T. K. "Cognitive Press in Computer-Mediated Work." In G. Salvendy, S. L. Sauter, and J. J. Hurrell, Jr. (eds.), *Social, Ergonomic, and Stress Aspects of Work with Computers.* Amsterdam: Elsevier, 1987.

Brown, J. S., Collins, A., and Duguid, P. "Situated Cognition and the Culture of Learning." *Educational Researcher,* 1988, *18,* 32–42.

Brown, J. S., and Duguid, P. "Enacting Design for the Workplace." In P. S. Adler and T. A. Winograd (eds.), *Usability: Turning Technologies into Tools.* New York: Oxford University Press, 1992.

Bullen, C. V., and Bennett, J. L. "Groupware in Practice: An Interpretation of Work Experiences." In C. Dunlop and R. Kling (eds.), *Computerization and Controversy: Value Conflicts and Social Choices.* Orlando, Fla.: Academic Press, 1991.

Cahoon, B. "Computer Skill Learning in the Workplace: A Comparative Case Study." Unpublished doctoral dissertation, University of Georgia, Athens, 1995.

Card, S. K., Moran, T. P., and Newell, A. *The Psychology of Human-Computer Interaction.* Hillsdale, N.J.: Erlbaum, 1983.

Carroll, J. M. *The Nurnberg Funnel: Designing Minimalist Instruction for Practical Computer Skill.* Cambridge, Mass.: MIT Press, 1990.

Cox, B. "Evolving a Distributed Learning Community." [http://www.virtualschool.edu:80/mon/Cox/OnlineClassroom.html]. Aug. 1996.

Crook, C. *Computers and the Collaborative Experience of Learning.* London: Routledge, 1994.

Czaja, S. J., Hammond, K., Blascovich, J. J., and Swede, H. "Learning to Use a Word-Processing System as a Function of Training Strategy." *Behaviour and Information Technology,* 1986, *5,* 203–216.

Czaja, S. J., Hammond, K., Blascovich, J. J., and Swede, H. "Age Related Differences in Learning to Use a Text-Editing System." *Behaviour and Information Technology,* 1989, *8,* 309–319.

Gattiker, U. E. "Computer Skills Acquisition: A Review and Future Directions for Research." *Journal of Management,* 1992, *18,* 547–574.

Gist, M. E., Rosen, B., and Schwoerer, C. "The Influence of Training Method and Trainee Age on the Acquisition of Computer Skills." *Personnel Psychology,* 1988, *41,* 255–265.

Gist, M. E., Schwoerer, C., and Rosen, B. "Effects of Alternative Training Methods on Self-Efficacy and Performance in Computer Software Training." *Journal of Applied Psychology,* 1989, *74,* 884–891.

Hutchins, E. L. *Cognition in the Wild.* Cambridge, Mass.: MIT Press, 1995.

Landauer, T. K. *The Trouble with Computers: Usefulness, Usability, and Productivity.* Cambridge, Mass.: MIT Press, 1995.

Lave, J., and Wenger, E. *Situated Learning: Legitimate Peripheral Participation.* New York: Cambridge University Press, 1991.

McGrath, J. E., and Hollingshead, A. B. *Groups Interacting with Technology: Ideas, Evidence, Issues, and an Agenda.* Thousand Oaks, Calif.: Sage, 1994.

Olsten Forum for Information Management. *Managing Today's Automated Workplace: A Special Report.* Westbury, N.Y.: Olsten Corporation, 1993.

Singley, M. K., and Anderson, J. R. *The Transfer of Cognitive Skill.* Cambridge, Mass.: Harvard University Press, 1989.

Waern, Y. *Cognitive Aspects of Computer Supported Tasks.* New York: Wiley, 1989.

Winer, D. "Frontier Community Center." [http://www.scripting.com/frontier/]. Aug. 1996.

Woolley, D. R. "Conferencing on the World Wide Web." [http://freenet.msp.mn.us/people/drwool/webconf.html]. Aug. 1996.

*BRAD CAHOON is coordinator for technology-based instruction at the Georgia Center for Continuing Education, University of Georgia, Athens.*

*A framework for transforming existing practitioner groups into inquiry communities is presented. Development occurs across the dimensions of intention, order, community, and voice.*

# Transforming Groups: Developing Practitioner Inquiry Communities

*Cassandra Drennon, Diane L. Foucar-Szocki*

When groups of teachers actively explore their practice together over time, the results can be powerfully transforming for those teachers, their learners, and their programs. Inspired by the possibilities, more and more leaders in adult literacy education have begun fostering practitioner inquiry communities as an approach to both staff development and program improvement. Many of these efforts have been enormously influenced by the work of Susan Lytle and her colleagues at the National Center on Adult Literacy (NCAL), who, throughout the early 1990s, published a series of technical reports advancing what they refer to as "practitioner inquiry" and "inquiry-based staff development" (Lytle, Belzer, and Reumann, 1992, 1993). In this chapter, we explore how, in such groups, practitioners learn through inquiry. First, we look at how learning is occurring in the Georgia Adult Literacy Practitioner Inquiry Network (GALPIN), a group formed first and foremost for the purpose of pursuing inquiry. Then, we contrast this with an experience in Virginia, where a group of practitioners has come together mainly to produce a product but has evolved over time into an inquiry community. Through this example, we introduce what we believe to be the most salient dimensions of inquiry—intention, order, community, and voice—suggesting that attention to and understanding of these dimensions will encourage more inquiry-based staff development practices within the field. We conclude with an invitation to all adult educators to overcome barriers to implementing practitioner inquiry by taking note of groups that already exist and developing them along each of these dimensions to become thriving inquiry communities that improve both individual practice and overall programs.

## The Character of Practitioner Inquiry Groups

According to Lytle, Belzer, and Reumann (1993), practitioner inquiry is best understood not so much as a set of activities or sequence of steps but as a questioning stance that teachers and administrators adopt toward their practice and a critical perspective they apply toward the larger social, cultural, and political contexts of literacy work. Certainly, individuals can adopt an inquiry stance toward their practice, asking and pursuing questions on their own without input or support from other colleagues. However, here we are speaking about inquiry as a group activity. The ultimate power of inquiry-based staff development resides in the unified voice and collective action that can emerge when practitioners collaboratively develop and express their ideas. On a lesser scale, groups are particularly well-suited for inquiry, because the group structure engenders collaborative learning and thereby reduces the isolation that often typifies adult literacy education. Practitioners working with groups of colleagues have the benefit of immediate feedback on their ideas from peers. Learning is enriched as group members draw on the skills and perspectives each brings. As individuals learn, so learns the entire group.

Inquiry is an approach to staff development and program improvement embodying a specific ideology of knowledge, power, and authority. Knowledge in inquiry groups is largely derived from inside programs by practitioners investigating their day-to-day practice together. This stands in contrast to more traditional training models of staff development that deliver knowledge generated by university researchers and content specialists from the outside.

Characteristically, decision-making power in inquiry groups is shared among the participants. Staff developers working with these groups guide the process of inquiry but do not generally direct the content of the group's work. As the group carries out its work, hierarchical relationships such as might exist among administrators and teachers or between experienced and less experienced teachers are diminished in varying degrees. This happens as group members pool their diverse knowledge, perspectives, and skills in the effort to understand more deeply issues of shared concern. Often, there is a high degree of participation among group members in planning for and managing their activities. Authority shifts from experts outside the program to practitioners inside the program who come to develop and articulate theories grounded in their real-world experience. Next, we describe two examples of inquiry groups in action—one formed for the purpose of inquiry and another that was transformed into an inquiry community over time.

## An Inquiry Group Formed

The Georgia Adult Literacy Practitioner Inquiry Network (GALPIN) is an example of a group organized for the express purpose of supporting inquiry. Literacy teachers and administrators were recruited to participate in the GALPIN project, based on their desire to engage in the process of inquiry as a form of staff development, not knowing what might actually emerge as the content of their inquiry. The group, funded by a private foundation grant, meets several times over a two-year period for intensive two-day retreats.

Through talk, the eighteen GALPIN participants first explored with one another the strengths as well as the tensions and dissonance they experienced as literacy practitioners. Out of these discussions, they began to frame individual and collective problems and then to identify questions that they were inspired to explore more deeply and systematically. Through more talk, reflection, journal writing, and other structured group activities, they worked together to unearth their tacit beliefs and assumptions surrounding the chosen issues. They looked within their practice to understand what was going on, how things seemed to happen, and why. In many instances, they also tried to gain perspective on the ways their dilemmas were shaped by social, cultural, and political circumstances. Many turned their attention for a time to the academic literature and research related to their areas of concern but then considered what they were reading in relation to their lived experience. Usually, practitioners used qualitative and quantitative research methods in their regular settings to study their questions systematically. These methods included classroom observations, surveys, interviews with adult learners, and analysis of student work and other documents. They studied the data they collected alone, with colleagues in the group, and even with the help of adult learners. These steps led many of the participants to refine their theories or make some practical change in their teaching, the effects of which have become the focus for further research.

One practitioner in the GALPIN project has documented dramatic increases in reading comprehension and reading enjoyment among adult learners who participated as co-researchers in her inquiry project. Ann had been teaching the same core group of students for nearly two years. Throughout that time, she had read extensively about methods for teaching reading and had experimented with a wide array of strategies. Reading test scores among her students, however, improved little. Ann became curious and concerned when she learned from her students that none of them read outside of class for purpose or pleasure. At GALPIN meetings, Ann talked about the reading situation with others and decided to pursue what seemed the simple question, "What will happen if my students regularly read at home?" Learners in her class agreed to spend some time every day at home reading for pleasure and to keep a log in which they recorded what they read, how much time they spent reading, and how they felt about what they read.

At the end of three months, the eight adults in Ann's class had logged more than three hundred hours of leisure reading. Each of the learners participating in Ann's project showed significant gains in reading comprehension. Ann and the students were most impressed, however, by the enthusiasm for reading that was engendered in everyone by the project. One learner told Ann, "I love reading now. I didn't before." Another reported, "The more books I read, the better I could read." Now the learners in Ann's class enthusiastically take responsibility for choosing books that the program will order, and they are all active users of the class library.

Another GALPIN participant, Rylan, applied her own interest in creative visualization to her General Educational Development (GED) classroom. She found the means to replace the school-type desks in her classroom with office desks. She took a Polaroid photo of each learner in a graduation cap and gown, which students framed and placed on their desks. Additionally, she devoted several fifteen-minute sessions each day between periods of instruction for students to stop what they were doing and visualize themselves going through the GED graduation ceremony or else working in their chosen field. Regularly, she had the students writing vivid accounts of their future lives. At first, Rylan's students thought the idea was silly but agreed to go along with it.

Over the course of several months, Rylan realized that learners were no longer dropping out of the program the way they did in the past. It used to be that she would lose nearly half the adults who came into her class over any given ten-week session. Through word of mouth, more and more adults began enrolling in her class, and more than 90 percent of these attended regularly throughout the whole session. The GED completion rate among learners who participated in the creative visualization project nearly doubled, too. Rylan is not convinced at this point that creative visualization is the reason things seem to be going so much better in her class lately. But she is convinced that she is on to something good and worthwhile. Her enthusiasm for teaching has been rejuvenated, and she believes that she is much more effective with students because of that.

Ann's and Rylan's experiences are rich examples of what occurs when practitioners explore their practice as members of an inquiry group. In both cases, the women involved colleagues in taking a close fresh look at classroom issues. Group members helped Ann and Rylan design their research projects and choose the methods they would use to collect data. After Ann and Rylan collected their data, group members helped them make sense of it all. All members of the inquiry group presented the results of their projects to one another and received more help at that point in refining their theories. The whole group is currently planning a symposium to which teachers and program administrators from around Georgia will be invited. They will come hear what group members have experienced through the year-long process of inquiry. Group members are now collaboratively writing chapters of a booklet, which the group will publish, documenting the process of inquiry. As they extend their learning to broader audiences in this way, others may come to appreciate the process of inquiry and benefit from their research efforts.

## A Group Transformed:
## Developing Dimensions of Inquiry

In addition to establishing and supporting inquiry communities like GALPIN—communities designed for the express purpose of inquiry—we suggest that many existing groups have the potential to develop into thriving inquiry communities, whether they begin as cliques, committees, planning teams, or something else. Likewise over time, structures in place such as planning periods, lunch gatherings, staff meetings, and study groups can be transformed into dynamic sites of inquiry. And practitioners in any stage of their development as professionals may make up the membership of groups seeking to function as inquiry communities. In short, it is possible for a group to start where its members are and then develop as an inquiry community. This development occurs across four interdependent dimensions of inquiry—intention, order, community, and voice.

Increasingly in education, we find groups forming for a myriad of purposes—to design curriculum, to solve a problem, to meet requirements instituted by the local or state education agency, or to better understand a situation or an environment. In education and elsewhere, the value of collective efforts continues to gain credibility.

**Intention.** Any purpose, or *intention,* for coming together can lead to inquiry—to a situation in which questions are pursued and assumptions challenged. Consider, for instance, a group of adult literacy practitioners in Virginia who have been charged with bringing about a new training curriculum for beginning adult basic education (ABE) teachers in that state. One of the first steps this group took was to invite in a national expert to present a model training program for new teachers that was being used in other states. Conceivably, this group could have carried out its task without question. Group members could have devoted their time to the mechanics of adopting and disseminating the content of the model training program. The group, however, intentionally moved toward inquiry, as it began to ask questions about the underlying assumptions of the task—wondering what role this curriculum would take in the group's own setting, and about the values that were implied through the curriculum, and how those related to the culture and values of learners served by the program. Such a stance reframed the work for greater understanding, meaning, and value for everyone involved. Learning occurred as the questions were explored and the work pursued. A meaningful transformation of the task began to occur.

Groups designed to honor and incorporate the perspectives of all members form the foundation for inquiry. In the initial stages of its work, the Virginia group established the norm that each member would commit to the group and to the success of its members. Group members were then able to say, "no one owned the project, but everyone owned it." The group intentionally designed its work so that each group member could find meaning in the individual as well as the collective efforts. Although the group's work has been facilitated, at times in fact directed, by a staff development specialist, there exists within the group what members describe as an ethos of equality that values as legitimate the circumstances, context, and perspectives of everyone.

It is not enough for someone external to the group—in this case a state education agency—to have an intention for it. In inquiry, the group must retain a large degree of decision-making authority, embracing its own intention and shaping the direction of its collective and individual work. The extent to which this can occur is subject to external expectations and constraints. If the group is charged with achieving an end that cannot be altered or adjusted within the group's ongoing work, it is not an inquiry group. If all decisions regarding purpose and direction are made outside the group or by one member of the group, this is not an inquiry group but something else. In our example, therefore, a movement toward inquiry within the group required that the state education agency requesting the work value the expertise that group members brought to the task. It required that the group's facilitator mediate the interests of the state and the group's own knowledge, skills, insights, abilities, and values.

Intention also includes a deliberate willingness to pursue questions or issues through to a meaningful conclusion. A group, for instance, that comes together each month to talk about its members' practice without any intention of following through on the questions in any systematic way exhibits intention and inquiry but lacks follow-through. Effective inquiry communities commit to following through on their work in a systematic and orderly way. Examples of intentional groups include book discussion groups, curriculum development efforts, teacher research projects, and school improvement teams. These stand in contrast to incidental groups that include, for example, teacher hallway talk, conference talk, and lunch talk. These are settings where often powerful questions about practice come up but are then rarely pursued with the intention of systematic follow-through.

**Order.** *Order* refers to the systematic ways that groups go about the business of inquiry, particularly in the realm of collecting and making sense of data. The notion of collecting data in an orderly and systematic way contrasts with "taking in" one's surroundings more casually and incidentally. Order emerges when the group commits to collecting the data over time, often a designated period of time. Anchoring work in the literature of the field further enhances order. The literature highlights what others think regarding a particular issue. Observations and data gathering are illuminated by a larger set of experiences and research recorded by others interested in similar questions.

The practitioners in Virginia who designed a new teacher training program elected to first collect data among themselves by reflecting on and writing about what they knew constituted good teaching and effective learning. Then they collected and analyzed academic readings on the subject of teacher training, looking for the assumptions embedded in those texts. They worked together to negotiate a philosophy that would, from that point on, guide their decisions about new teacher training. After the national expert came and presented the model training program to them, they related the philosophy of that training to what they had developed as their own. Next, the group wrote its own training materials, drawing on all of these sources. Members struggled among themselves to negotiate a curriculum reflecting the knowledge and values of the group.

Order also includes a commitment to gather evidence to which practitioners and others can see and respond. The group in Virginia presented a draft of its training model to forums of practitioners around the state and collected more data. This time, the group was asking the question, "Do ABE practitioners in Virginia find our training model compatible with their own beliefs about what constitutes good adult learning principles?" Members collected data in the form of written and anecdotal reactions to their work. They returned to the inquiry group to study the data they had collected, then continued to shape the training model to incorporate new discoveries.

The range and richness of questions generated through practitioner inquiry groups matures over time. To some practitioners in particular settings or contexts, an application-oriented question such as, What should be the content of a New ABE Teacher Training program? is a significant question. However, deeper questions may emerge over time. This was the case as Virginia practitioners studied whether their work was philosophically compatible among practitioners who were diverse in terms of race, gender, geography, and teaching context. It is the increasing commitment to the orderly gathering and analysis of data over time and the sharing with others that heightens the inquiry. Thus, an inquiry group cannot be judged solely by the type of question that brings it together but rather by how the members pursue the intention that brings them together. The key features are the intention to seek answers to questions that emerge from practice, to pursue understanding through ordered data-gathering strategies, and to do so as a community of learners—together, not alone.

**Community.** *Community* refers to the culture within groups. In inquiry-based staff development, community is developed through the collective struggle that comes from clarifying intent and order. Inquiry invites educators to experience the richness of their work. It affords a forum whereby practitioners can ask their own questions, seek their own answers, and actively participate in unraveling the complexities of teaching and learning. Moving from being a group of educators with something in common to an inquiry community takes time, trust, shared purpose, commitment, struggle, and mutual recognition.

Communities are born of unity in diversity. A group becomes community as the whole becomes greater than the sum of parts and as each member relies on others in ways previously unimagined. A group becomes community when that which members share goes beyond completing the task or answering the question to a shared ownership that honors all members equally and sees the work as significant for its own sake. The potential for a group of individuals to develop into community is enhanced or obstructed as decisions are made along the way. The staff development specialist in Virginia told us that her own stance toward inquiry guided her early decision to transfer ownership of the project to practitioners. In contrast, she could have defined the group merely as an advisory committee—seeking members' input but then ultimately designing a teacher training curriculum according to her own best judgment or that of the national expert. Her stance toward inquiry further enabled particular norms to develop within the group; members increasingly embraced their ownership of the project because, in this case, they were freed to do so.

Groups develop into inquiry communities by the stances exhibited toward one another's work. As the Virginia teachers grew to value the questions of their colleagues and worked to create safe spaces for those questions to be pursued, explored, and shared—they became, in effect, an inquiry-based community of professionals. Sustaining community is not always easy in groups, however. In Virginia, the group's sense of community has been threatened during periods when conflicting values about the training program have arisen. At times, intentionality regarding follow-through has wavered among some group members also. In these cases, strong norms within the larger group have kept the work on course. Members' commitment to honor diversity in the context of shared purpose provides the compass that somehow guides them through difficult times.

**Voice.** *Voice* refers to the extent and ways that the knowledge constructed within inquiry groups is made increasingly more public. The notion of voice contrasts with the traditions that have long silenced teachers. There is great benefit to learners and to the profession when practitioners write and speak publicly about what they know. Many inquiry communities develop a strong sense of voice, recognizing and valuing the contribution that can be made by entering the professional discourse.

Voice, like the other features of inquiry, is exhibited in varying degrees. If we return once again to our group in Virginia that has slowly transformed itself into an inquiry community, what would we expect? Because they are a community, members have been sharing among themselves, refining what they now know, and discussing what they will do as a result of their new knowledge. They are now coming to an increasing realization that they have learned something worth sharing with an even broader audience—other state agencies in Virginia and ABE staff developers in other states. The step of sharing beyond the community is not an easy one to take, however. Some members are uncomfortable, suggesting that discussion among themselves is sufficient. However, others feel that if the group were to stop here, its members would experience a disappointing lack of closure.

Initially, inquiry participants may be satisfied with the internal recognition that they have a legitimate perspective. Sharing within the group is the next step. Recognition and assurance within the group lead to a commitment by the group to support advancing the ideas to a larger circle through discussion, writing, and speaking. Individual group members or the group itself may advance individual or collective voices. They may choose to write collectively, in pairs, or individually—presenting results locally, regionally, statewide, or nationally—as the power of their voice matures. Voice therefore, represents one more dimension across which groups may choose to move. Our experience suggests that those who work in groups that extend their voices beyond their own sphere of influence become stronger proponents for teachers and learners alike. These voices improve quality in practice.

Along with speaking comes listening. The practitioners in the Virginia inquiry group have come to listen more attentively to their own inner voice, their students' voices, and the voices of their fellow practitioners in an effort to enhance understanding and achievement. Having more voices ought not to create a cacophony of unrelated noise but rather a symphony of integrated sound. Leaders, policy makers, and others play a role in taking what might be feared as potentially dissonant, in-harmonic chatter and organizing it into a full chorus, replete with the breadth and depth of all participants. It is our obligation to create the spaces that allow the voices of adult literacy educators to fill our classrooms, hallways, conferences, retreats, policies, journals, and books. These voices, formed from pursuing an inquiry stance toward their work, advance us all.

## Facing Challenges to Inquiry

With budget cutbacks and a national movement toward greater accountability, many adult education leaders consider altering traditional staff development programs now to be a daunting task. Practitioners and staff developers alike voice concern that inquiry is simply a time-consuming process of recreating the wheel rather than an efficient means for acquiring practical teaching strategies that work. Some are concerned as well about what they perceive to be a competing agenda within the group to critique the very structures that provide their employment. On the one hand, administrators worry that individuals within a group may focus too narrowly, deriving outcomes that do not truly enhance programs. On the other hand, the same administrators may be concerned that inquiry will inspire change efforts that the larger program is not ready to take on (Drennon, 1994). In these cases, the reason often given for not supporting inquiry is that it simply is not cost effective.

It is precisely because of these concerns that we practitioners must diligently pursue practitioner inquiry as a vehicle for transforming our field. Inquiry-based staff development suggests a new approach for both professional development and program improvement through group learning. It provides us with a vehicle to better understand and serve our field from the inside out and to inform those on the outside about what truly matters, while achieving meaningful accountability.

To do this, we suggest that, in addition to forming groups deliberately for inquiry, existing groups can also be transformed into inquiry communities. Transforming an existing group means providing an environment in which questions can be pursued and assumptions challenged—a group can move from passively accepting and pursuing an externally defined purpose to actively questioning the underlying assumptions of the purpose and pursuing systematically to a logical end that might or might not achieve what the group was originally convened to do.

## Conclusion

To better facilitate this move toward inquiry, we have attended to four dimensions—intention, order, community, and voice—keeping in mind that while we have presented these dimensions as distinct, we do so only to enhance understanding. We recognize that these are not necessarily mutually exclusive categories but rather identifiable features of inquiry that grow, one from the other. We encourage further research and discussion of their saliency. Further, we believe that deliberate attention to fostering development across these dimensions provides practitioners with a starting point for infusing inquiry into existing staff development and program improvement efforts.

It is through greater intention and order, a stronger sense of community, and greater voice that groups can be transformed into thriving inquiry communities that improve both practice and programs. Inquiry has the potential to characterize the culture of an educational workplace and to evolve into a professional way of life for practitioners. Let us aspire to actively develop such communities, where all of us—learners, teachers, aides, administrators, staff developers, and policy-makers—can learn, contribute, belong, and make a difference.

# References

Drennon, C. *Adult Literacy Practitioners as Researchers.* ERIC Digest. Washington, D.C.: National Clearinghouse for Literacy Education, Center for Applied Linguistics, 1994. (ED 372 663)

Lytle, S. L., Belzer, A., and Reumann, R. *Invitations to Inquiry: Rethinking Staff Development in Adult Literacy Education.* Technical Report TR92–2. Philadelphia: National Center on Adult Literacy, 1992.

Lytle, S. L., Belzer, A., and Reumann, R. *Initiating Practitioner Inquiry: Adult Literacy Teachers, Tutors, and Administrators Research Their Practice.* Technical Report TR93–11. Philadelphia: National Center on Adult Literacy, 1993.

CASSANDRA DRENNON *is a doctoral student in adult education at the University of Georgia, Athens, and co-facilitator of the Georgia Adult Literacy Practitioner Inquiry Network.*

DIANE L. FOUCAR-SZOCKI *is president of DFS Associates in Harrisonburg, Virginia, a private educational consulting and research organization. She serves on the faculty of the National Creative Problem-Solving Institute.*

*Hundreds of thousands of adults participate in book discussion groups, satisfying lifelong learning needs informally and in community.*

# Book Groups: Communities of Learners

*Sandra Kerka*

According to O'Connor (1991), "In the late 19th and early 20th centuries, hundreds of thousands of American men and women, mostly women, participated in locally or nationally organized reading circles or study circles" (p. 334). In the late twentieth century, this is still true. Having waxed and waned, the popularity of book discussion groups has again peaked in the last two decades. Although there is no way to determine the exact numbers of adult participants, there is evidence of a great deal of activity. Numerous guides and manuals for book groups have appeared recently (Jacobsohn, 1994; Laskin and Hughes, 1995; Pearlman, 1994; Saal, 1995; Slezak, 1993). A search of *Newspaper Abstracts* turns up articles in the *San Francisco Chronicle, Denver Post, New York Times, Boston Globe, Detroit News, Los Angeles Times, Atlanta Constitution,* and *St. Louis-Post Dispatch* documenting the growth of book groups all over the United States. Publishers such as Doubleday, HarperCollins, and Penguin regularly issue reading group companions to new books, sometimes available free at bookstores. Large chains such as Barnes & Noble and Borders, smaller bookstores, and libraries lend their support by organizing and providing space for group meetings, ensuring the availability of multiple copies, and distributing reading lists (Balcom, 1992; Kinsella, 1993; Mutter, 1995; Saal, 1995).

Book groups have a long history. Women's reading groups were organized by Aspasia in Athens, Greece, and by St. Jerome in Rome (O'Connor, 1991). Literary discussions took place in the salons of Paris and the coffee houses of London. Anne Hutchinson drew the wrath of Puritan authorities with her women's discussion groups. However, she began an American tradition that continued throughout the nineteenth century with the Boston bluestockings and women's literary circles, including those established by freed African

American women and Catholic women (Laskin and Hughes, 1995; O'Connor, 1991). The Great Books Movement, which was begun in Chicago in 1929, spread nationally after World War II, injecting new energy into the phenomenon. The National Endowment for the Humanities funded the "Let's Talk About It" program in the late 1980s (Balcom, 1992). Many threads led to today's book group explosion, among them consciousness-raising groups organized during the women's movement in the 1960s and 1970s (Neidorf, 1995), an increase in the number of college-educated people in the population, and possibly an end-of-the-century search for community and meaning (Laskin and Hughes, 1995).

Book groups have diverse forms and purposes. Teachers often form them in order to reflect with colleagues on teaching and learning (Flood and others, 1994; Pelletier, 1993). Older adults in institutional settings can improve mental functioning through reading clubs (Palmore, 1986). Parents organize them either with children to encourage reading (Slezak, 1993) or with other parents to evaluate children's literature and discuss ways to help their children read (Simic and Macfarlane, 1995). Adult basic education reading groups are promoted as a way to overcome the isolation of adult new readers and to create learning communities that will support and sustain their newly acquired skills (District of Columbia Public Library, 1993). Even as some claim that the cyber age portends the end of the book, the Internet teems with discussion groups for mysteries, science fiction, and other genres. On the World Wide Web, the GNN (Global Navigator Network) Story Café distributes Mickey Pearlman's advice for starting book groups (Jaquette, 1996), and the Virtual Reading Group provides a place for those who have not been able to join real-time reading groups due to time constraints or relocations (Sherman, 1996).

In this chapter, the characteristics of today's adult book groups are discussed, exploring why people join and who participates. The nature of the learning that occurs in book groups is described, and some implications for adult education are considered. The literature contains many studies of classroom book discussions with children and adolescents but little research on adult reading groups. However, there is a great deal of anecdotal material from book group members in the recently published guides mentioned earlier. These testimonies were used as case study material, fleshing out this portrait of book discussion groups.

## Nature of Contemporary Book Groups

Why do people join book groups? "Reading is a solitary activity, but book groups are all about community" (Neidorf, 1995, p. 67). Reading groups seem to satisfy deep needs, judging by the way people talk about them: "I come because it keeps me sane" (Neidorf, 1995, p. 67); "My book group has been a signpost for my life. . . . Our book group is our life support. . . . My book club has saved my life" (Slezak, 1993); "I can't imagine life without a book group" (Jacobsohn, 1994). The group members surveyed by Jacobsohn (1994), Laskin and Hughes (1995), and Slezak (1993) express a need for intelligent conversation, an outlet not fulfilled by other aspects of adults' busy lives. For some, it is a need for purposeful community, for connectedness that overcomes the isolating factors of contemporary life (Pearlman, 1994). Although the reading and discussion are central, the social aspect is also very important in most groups. Essayists in Slezak's book mention the following motives for participation: the discipline of reading by a deadline, the emotional satisfaction of having one's opinions validated, and the exposure to books and ideas not otherwise encountered. "Today's book clubs have lost some of the high mindedness and cultural voracity of groups in the past.... The cultural insecurity that drove a lot of people to join Great Books groups has also waned" (Laskin and Hughes, 1995, p. 16).

Talk is one of the ways through which human beings make meaning. Moore (1994) describes conversation as performing a pleasurable alchemy on experience, sublimating it into forms that can be examined. Book group members often refer to their book talk as alchemy, "transforming raw untempered thoughts into finer materials" (Slezak, 1993, p. 9). As Brookfield (1986) says, "to participate in discussion—in the collaborative externalization, exploration, and critical analysis of personally significant meaning systems—is to realize one's adulthood to its fullest extent" (p. 140).

Groups are composed of all women, all men, or both. A few specialize in specific types of books (for example, works by women or by African American authors) or have defined membership (lesbians or gay men, alumni of a particular institution, writers or poets, or teachers). The composition of the group is a crucial element. Diversity is an essential ingredient in ensuring a broad discussion that reflects many viewpoints. Finding that others love a book as much as you do is satisfying, but disagreement usually leads to a livelier discussion, one with greater potential for learning. "Adults were far more interested in exploring difference than they were in reaching consensus" (Marshall, Smagorinsky, and Smith, 1995, p. 112).

Some groups try to mix different ages, occupations, social circles, and cultural backgrounds. A healthy group seeks a balance between similarity and difference, between a safe, nonthreatening environment with like members and the expanded perspective provided by those with varied backgrounds (Jacobsohn, 1994). The pluralism of the group ensures that there are both shared values, common goals, and identification as a group, as well as disparate values—because each person is a member of multiple other subcultures beyond the book group (Heimlich and Norland, 1994).

Having said that, it should be noted that the vast majority of participants in book groups are women, and all-women groups outnumber all-men groups, according to the mostly anecdotal evidence. Varied reasons are given for this phenomenon. "Women have always had to create their own intellectual societies" (Neidorf, 1995, p. 64). In the days of Aspasia and Anne Hutchinson as well as the Chautauqua Literary and Scientific Circle and other nineteenth-century women's clubs, women who were denied access to higher education hungered for intellectual and cultural society. (See Chapter One for further discussion of women's learning groups.) Even now, when many women are college educated, they still seek verification of their experience and understanding of the world in communal settings. In the past, women often came together for common purposes related to household production tasks. Now, "talking about books is a way of quilting, of weaving together the threads of our lives" (Slezak, 1993, p. 96). Women are supposed to be more comfortable with sharing their inner lives and personal experiences, more driven by the need for connection, and likely to prefer a noncompetitive atmosphere for intellectual activity (Pearlman, 1994; Saal, 1995).

Laskin and Hughes (1995) suggest that the differences in the types of discussion that go on in all-women and mixed groups are considerable. A woman in Bauman's (1994) study states that in women-only discussions, "there wasn't much to talk about . . . we all pretty much agreed with each other or felt awkward challenging each other" (p. 34). However, Neidorf (1995) and many of Slezak's essay contributors (1993) found that women-only groups offer considerable stimulation, challenge, and depth, as well as an environment in which they felt comfortable with speaking freely.

Another characteristic on which groups diverge is leadership. The majority of groups are member-led; in many, an unofficial, unstructured type of leadership gets discussion started, keeps it on track, and ensures equitable participation. Some groups share these facilitation tasks equally among members, taking turns in preparing background material and discussion questions and leading the book talk (Jacobsohn, 1994). Sometimes co-leaders are designated to share this pre- and during-meeting workload.

Other groups, especially those organized by libraries and alumni associations or affiliated with the Great Books Foundation, are always led by official presenters, often teachers, librarians, writers, or book critics. Paid professionals such as Rachel Jacobsohn (1994) facilitate discussions for multiple groups. People who feel strongly about having designated leaders or presenters believe it is essential to have structure in order to have a focused and productive discussion. Others value the self-direction and un-school-like atmosphere of a group "run on the principles of democracy taken to their logical extreme—loosely bridled chaos" (Slezak, 1993, p. 114). Obviously, there is no single recipe for a successful group; each one has its own spirit, soul, and style (Saal, 1995).

## Adult Learning in Book Groups

Three factors that affect learning are people, structure, and culture (Merriam and Caffarella, 1991). Diversity of the people in the group is an important element. All the how-to manuals address the issues of what kinds of people to include, optimal group size, and how to add members carefully. As Heimlich and Norland (1994) note, changes in membership can alter a group's personality and dynamics. Commitment and participation are also vital to the learning that takes place. Members who do not finish the book or actively participate in the discussion are not supporting the learning of other group members (Jacobsohn, 1994).

As for group structure, Bauman (1994) points out that the quality of the learning experience is directly related to the informal context of reading groups. The loose structure mentioned earlier and the typical physical arrangement of seating in a circle enhance the sense of equal status among members, creating a comfortable, safe atmosphere in which participants feel free to share ideas, feelings, and disagreement about the book, not personal conflicts. At the same time, whether there are designated leaders or not, whether groups have no rules or many, the central activity of all groups is down-to-business focused dialogue about the book.

Culture is another factor influencing learning. All groups of learners form learning communities with unique minicultures, determined by the group's subconscious belief system, values, and attitudes about the dominant culture (Heimlich and Norland, 1994). Book groups fit the characteristics of a learning community: they are artificially formed, their behavior is for specific purposes, newcomers must demonstrate their worthiness to belong, and they form a network of support. A theme of many of Slezak's essayists (1993) is the support that members derive from their groups. For example, one woman explains that taking on the challenge of books that are denser in language, structure, and thought requires a sort of intellectual support group. Successful book groups must also display the characteristics of group cohesion: commitment to the group's goals, conformity to the group's norms, loyalty, acceptance of responsibility, increased communication among members, willingness to be influenced by group members, and acceptance of others' opinions (Cranton, 1994). Cohesiveness enables groups to operate smoothly and solidifies the atmosphere in which learning can take place.

Book groups also have the characteristics of learning networks identified by Brookfield (1986): groups united by a common concern or agreed-upon purpose that exchange information, ideas, skills, and knowledge and create new forms of knowledge. According to Jacobsohn (1994), they do this "by combining individual strengths in personality and areas of knowledge . . . the group becomes smarter and more effective than the sum of the individuals" (p. 64).

What kinds of learning take place in book groups? Marshall, Smagorinsky, and Smith (1995) list five kinds of knowledge to be gained from literature: knowledge of texts, of contexts, of self, of others, and of how to read.

*Knowledge of texts.* Obviously, the reader can learn a great deal from the book itself: context and background, subject matter, technique, characters, symbols, theme, and style. In a group, members share this knowledge with each other, as well as that acquired in preparatory research they may have done on the author, the period, existing criticism of the work, and so on.

*Knowledge of contexts.* Analysis of the communication processes in reading groups (Flood and others, 1994; Marshall, Smagorinsky, and Smith, 1995; Swanson, 1993) shows that a variety of group process skills are acquired and used during book discussions: gatekeeping, diagnosing problems, compromising, harmonizing, building consensus, giving and seeking information, coordinating, recording, and expediting. Formal and informal group leaders acquire and enhance facilitation skills while handling disagreements, dealing with participants who monopolize the discussion or digress extensively, and negotiating which books are to be read.

*Knowledge of self and others.* Personal and interpersonal growth is one of the most important aspects of learning in book groups. "For members of reading groups, stylistics and structure matter much less than do believable characters that can provide them with meaningful moral or psychological insights" (Long, 1987, p. 306). Marshall, Smagorinsky, and Smith (1995) similarly found that adult discussions emphasized an ethical dimension. Book groups provide a context in which individuals can change their value frameworks, moral codes, and cultural constructs (Bauman, 1994).

A recurrent theme in the literature is the value of connecting texts and life. According to Jacobsohn (1994), reading at the end of the twentieth century is no longer a means of reinforcing traditional values or escaping from everyday life but of understanding life and the world. Long (1987) terms this "reading and reading the culture," an echo of Freire's definition of literacy as reading the word and the world. Through interaction with other readers who have different sources of knowledge and experience, group members can acquire other lenses through which to view and interpret texts as well as to integrate and understand their own experiences. The teachers in Flood and others' study (1994) were able to transcend cultural boundaries and see similarities with characters from different cultures. Those of the same ethnicity as the author or the characters could choose to play the role of expert and contribute their specific cultural knowledge to the group. With different lenses, members can read critically—for example, seeing which character is profiting in a situation (Slezak, 1993). The blend of social and intellectual activity that is characteristic of most groups allows members to use both textual and personal sources of knowledge to construct new meanings (Swanson, 1993), although Marshall, Smagorinsky, and Smith (1995) found that women use personal sources more often; men use textual ones.

*How to read.* Metacognition can also be increased through book discussion. Both during discussion and in reflection afterward, participants analyze how they derive meaning from the text and compare it to others' ways of knowing. Bauman (1994) describes this as reeducating themselves about how they and others think. A poetry group's essay (Slezak, 1993) reflects how a group becomes aware of how it reads, thinks, and learns, trying to achieve "that rare out-of-one's-self state attainable when we're struggling to understand on an intuitive level as well as a rational, intellectual one" (p. 40). Group membership exposes people to reading choices they might not otherwise have made and new ways to approach and interpret a text. As they experience that "a-ha, I never thought of it that way" feeling, they gain insights into themselves as learners—their learning preferences, tolerance for ambiguity, and self-knowledge are distilled through social interaction.

## Book Groups Are Not Like School

Another theme apparent in the literature is that reading groups are not like school. Reading group members remarked to Laskin and Hughes (1995) about how different their college classes were from the discussions in their groups. One said, "I want to discuss literature as a person, not as a student" (p. 23). "Book groups at their best are a bit like school without teachers, tests, or term papers—a kind of dream classroom where you can sip wine and nibble snacks" (p. xvii), freely relate characters to personal experience, and debunk literary pretensions. Balcom (1992) considers groups "more fun than school, no tests or grading" (p. 2), and Slezak (1993) calls them "tuition-free intellectual stimulation" (p. vi). Although there is an element of the mandatory in the expectation that members will attend and will finish the book, members are free to negotiate the curriculum in terms of choosing the texts they will read. Perhaps most disconcerting for adult educators is Saal's comment: "If the members wanted to be back in school, they would be taking a literature class in an adult education program rather than showing up at a reading group" (1995, p. 12).

What is it about the formal educational experience that inspires such comments? Bauman (1994) suggests that older adults dislike regimented educational formats and competitive, externally controlled programs. In book groups, "without the pressures of degree-oriented coursework or the costs and short duration of a continuing education course, members were free just to learn" (p. 36).

The dynamics of discussion are one way in which book groups differ from formal educational contexts. Several studies analyzing classroom communication looked at adult book groups in order to compare their discussion processes (Marshall, Smagorinsky, and Smith, 1995; Swanson, 1993). Their findings provide insights for both adult and elementary-secondary education. Swanson (1993) found that book club members speak slightly longer in each turn than do students in class. Club members tend to speak for an increasingly longer time as the discussion continues; classrooms are time bound and discussion must often be cut off arbitrarily when the time period ends. Swanson also found that teachers do not always cede control of meaning making to students. Personal knowledge is used more in book clubs than in class discussions. Club members tend to ask more "authentic" questions—those arising organically from the nature of the discussion; teachers tend to use more discussion-controlling questions. Turn taking is more fluid in book groups than in class (Marshall, Smagorinsky, and Smith, 1995), and group members use cooperative turns—helping others make a point or develop an idea—more often. Being a club member authorizes adults to speak, whereas in the classes studied, students must be invited to speak, and only the teacher is authorized to respond. Adult discussants do not shape their responses to the answers the teacher is looking for.

Marshall, Smagorinsky, and Smith (1995) compare classroom discussion to Bakhtin's notion of authoritative discourse: used in contexts of unequal power relations, it is rigid, demands acknowledgment, and is usually not transferred to other situations. Book discussion groups, in contrast, are characterized by internally persuasive discourse: participants internalize other voices, remain open to new contexts, and transfer the meanings they derive to other situations.

Another point of difference between academic environments and book groups is in the approaches to and uses of literature. Marshall, Smagorinsky, and Smith (1995) suggest that the culture of readers is not the same as the culture of literary critics and analysts. Long (1987) agrees that "reading occupies a very different place in the lives of academic and nonacademic readers" (p. 306). Book group members *can* read as literary critics do. For example, many groups refer to published reviews and examine a book as a piece of writing, looking at its stylistic and structural aspects and aesthetic value. However, these readers want a reading experience that is personally significant and enduring, using literature as a repository of values against which to shape and measure their own. In contrast to the classroom, Swanson (1993) often found adults engaging with the texts by recreating the characters' experiences for themselves and projecting their ideas of what the characters thought, a way of trying on different selves.

This way of using literature corresponds to Brookfield's definition (1986) of "nontechnical" adult learning, which is concerned with the resolution of moral difficulties, development of self-concept, capacity to explore other worldviews, reflection on experience, and evolution of personal ethical codes. These uses of literature have a value beyond self-development. Long (1987) says, "In living out the importance of ideas, in striving for self-understanding, as well as personal and social criticism, these groups, however limited by middle-class biases and perspectives, show that it is possible to work through some of those biases in the process of reflection on books" (p. 322). She suggests that these small-scale reformulations in participants' thinking are as necessary for social change as larger revolutions.

## Book Groups and Adult Education

The characteristics of book groups described here reflect a number of the principles of adult education: the groups incorporate a safe, accepting, inclusive environment; discussion as a learning method; learning as a social activity; personal experience as a legitimate source of knowledge; and critical reflection. However, this type of informal learning does not get a great deal of attention in research or in practice, despite the fact that it may be better suited to the needs of many adults who are not interested in acquiring credentials or whose geographic location or economic circumstances make participation in higher education difficult (Bauman, 1994).

Do adult educators have a role in this type of learning? An obvious role might be to form book groups as a staff development method for themselves or for other organizations. Adult educators could serve as brokers for the formation of learning networks, helping bring together past and former students or making information available about existing groups (Cranton, 1994). For book groups that desire a leader or presenter, adult educators who are skilled at group facilitation and armed with knowledge of learning styles could serve this function. Bauman (1994) makes the case that many institutions offer their customers only what they have to sell. He suggests that adult educators take a closer look at inexpensive, informal learning methods for those adults whose needs are best served in this way.

In *The Gutenberg Elegies,* Birkets (1994) ponders the fate of reading in an electronic age. The passionate commitment to reading by adults in book groups suggests that it may be too soon to declare the death of reading. Book groups fulfill the need for community and continuity in a constantly changing environment. The free expression of opinions and exchange of ideas—and the trust underlying both—are essential in a democratic society. While living in Slovakia, Willens (1994) found that no one would come to the book group she tried to organize because, under the former communist government, such meetings were dangerous places in which to expose one's ideological viewpoint. People had lost the habit of expressing personal opinions in public and were unable to engage in democratic debate and to test unorthodox ideas in the social crucible.

Constructivists believe that people "have two basic attributes, an innate and powerful drive to relate to others and a continuing attempt to make sense of their experiences" (Candy, 1991, p. 258). In book discussion groups, adults can satisfy both the need for relationship and for lifelong learning.

## References

Balcom, T. *Book Discussions for Adults: A Reader's Guide.* Chicago: American Library Association, 1992.

Bauman, P. "Book Groups: Informal and Innovative Adult Learning." *Journal of Adult Education,* 1994, 22 (2), 31–41.

Birkets, S. *The Gutenberg Elegies: The Fate of Reading in an Electronic Age.* Winchester, Mass.: Faber & Faber, 1994.

Brookfield, S. *Understanding and Facilitating Adult Learning: A Comprehensive Analysis of Principles and Effective Practices.* San Francisco: Jossey-Bass, 1986.

Candy, P. C. *Self-Direction for Lifelong Learning: A Comprehensive Guide to Theory and Practice.* San Francisco: Jossey-Bass, 1991.

Cranton, P. *Understanding and Promoting Transformative Learning: A Guide for Educators of Adults.* San Francisco: Jossey-Bass, 1994.

District of Columbia Public Library. *A Feel for Books: Book Discussions for Adult Developing*

*Readers. A Resource Manual.* Washington, D.C.: District of Columbia Public Library, 1993. (ED 364 260)

Flood, J., Lapp, D., Alvarez, D., Romero, A., Ranck-Buhr, W., Moore, J., Jones, M. A., Kabilids, C., and Lungren, L. *Teacher Book Clubs: A Study of Teachers' and Student Teachers' Participation in Contemporary Multicultural Fiction Literature Discussion Groups.* Athens, Ga., and College Park, Md.: National Reading Research Center, 1994. (ED 379 597)

Heimlich, J. E., and Norland, E. *Developing Teaching Style in Adult Education.* San Francisco: Jossey-Bass, 1994.

Jacobsohn, R. W. *The Reading Group Handbook.* New York: Hyperion, 1994.

Jaquette, V. "Reading Groups and Writing Women: An Interview with Mickey Pearlman." *GNN Story Café.* [http://gnn-e2a.gnn.com/gnn/meta/book/what/interview.html]. Apr. 1996.

Kinsella, B. "Reading Groups Get Publishers' Boost." *Publishers Weekly,* Oct. 4, 1993, pp. 18–19.

Laskin, D., and Hughes, H. *The Reading Group Book.* New York: Penguin Books, 1995.

Long, E. "Reading Groups and the Postmodern Crisis of Cultural Authority." *Cultural Studies,* 1987, *1* (3), 306–327.

Marshall, J. D., Smagorinsky, P., and Smith, S. W. *The Language of Interpretation: Patterns of Discourse in Discussions of Literature.* Urbana, Ill.: National Council of Teachers of English, 1995. (ED 374 466)

Merriam, S. B., and Caffarella, R. S. *Learning in Adulthood: A Comprehensive Guide.* San Francisco: Jossey-Bass, 1991.

Moore, T. *Soul Mates.* New York: HarperCollins, 1994.

Mutter, J. "Book Group Must-Read: 'Reading Group Choices.'" *Publishers Weekly,* Feb. 27, 1995, p. 32.

Neidorf, R. M. "Feminist Book Groups: The New C.R.?" *Ms.,* 1995, *5,* 65–67.

O'Connor, T. F. "American Catholic Reading Circles 1886–1909." *Libraries and Culture,* 1991, *26,* 334–347.

Palmore, S. N. "Senior Literary Circles: An Enrichment Program for Extended Care Facilities." *RQ,* 1986, *26,* 90–96. (ED 344 283)

Pearlman, M. *What to Read: The Essential Guide for Reading Group Members and Other Book Lovers.* New York: Harper Perennial, 1994.

Pelletier, C. M. "Professional Development Through a Teacher Book Club." Paper presented at the annual meeting of the American Educational Research Association, Atlanta, Apr. 1993. (ED 360 289)

Saal, R. *The New York Public Library Guide to Reading Groups.* New York: Crown, 1995.

Sherman, N. M. *Virtual Reading Group.* [http://velcome.iupui.edu/~nlsherman/Virtual.html]. Apr. 1996.

Simic, M. R., and Macfarlane, E. C. *Family Book Sharing Groups—Start One in Your Neighborhood!* Bloomington, Ind.: EDINFO Press and Family Literacy Center, 1995. (ED 374 401)

Slezak, E. *The Book Group Book: A Thoughtful Guide to Forming and Enjoying a Stimulating Book Discussion Group.* Chicago: Chicago Review Press, 1993.

Swanson, A. "Adult Book Club Discussions: Response as a Key." Paper presented at the annual meeting of the National Reading Conference, Charleston, S.C., Dec. 1993. (ED 364 837)

Willens, S. P. "Dangerous Book Clubs." *Belles Lettres,* 1994, *10* (1), 84–85.


*SANDRA KERKA is associate director of the ERIC Clearinghouse on Adult, Career, and Vocational Education, The Ohio State University, and is a participant in the learning communities of dance and quilting.*

*Common themes and issues emerging from discussions of learning in groups in the previous chapters are identified.*

# Summing Up: Themes and Issues Related to Learning in Groups

*Susan Imel*

With little support from research, learning in groups has been accepted as part of the woof and warp of adult education, with groups woven throughout many practice settings. As adult educators, we have undoubtedly formed theories about the use of groups and about how learning occurs in groups. Known as *theories-in-use*, they are what we tend to rely on when using groups in our practice. Whether tacit or expressed, these theories determine how we structure learning groups, as well as how we think about how learning happens in groups. Unless we take time to examine these theories, however, we probably remain unaware of how they influence our practice and whether they contain incongruities and inconsistencies (Argyris and Schön, 1977; Knights, 1993). One of the goals of this sourcebook is to provide opportunities for adult educators to surface, reflect on, and as appropriate, adjust their theories about learning in groups.

Previous chapters have examined some aspects of learning in groups and explored settings in which group learning occurs. In this last chapter, I weave together a number of themes that have appeared throughout the chapters and delineate some issues that have been raised. Future directions for adult learning groups are suggested in conclusion.

## Themes and Issues

Although they have examined different facets of learning in groups, the authors of the previous nine chapters have touched on a number of common themes and raised some issues related to groups in adult education. These themes and issues further clarify the status of learning in groups in adult education and also point to future directions for this area. The interrelated themes and issues I have selected for discussion include differing perceptions about learning in groups, the relationship of group process to content, the role of the facilitator, power relations in groups, and groups as communities of learners.

**Perceptions of Learning.** Because the nature of learning in groups is complex, the various chapters present a range of perspectives. Of particular interest are the varying ideas about the purpose of group learning. For example, does the group support and foster the learning of individual group members, or does the group as an entity learn? Most authors acknowledge the importance of the group and its members in helping shape knowledge, but the emphasis is primarily on the group as a vehicle that supports the learning of individuals. In Chapter Six, on learning in the workplace, however, West describes how the role of team learning in learning organizations is for the purpose of organizational transformation. In this setting, the stress is on the learning of the group as an entity. In discussing practitioner inquiry groups in Chapter Eight, Drennon and Foucar-Szocki use two examples from practice that depict how different learning emphases emerge from groups with similar goals: in one example, the group supported and fostered the learning of its individual members, whereas in the second, the focus was on the group's learning.

Perhaps the best way to view the conundrum about the type of learning supported and fostered by the group is to think of it as being on a continuum, with support for individual learning at one end and support for the group learning as an entity at the other. With some types of group learning—for example, cooperative learning as described by Cranton (Chapter Three)—the focus is explicitly on the learning of individual group members. As groups become more collaborative or transformative, however, the distinction between individual learning and group learning becomes more transparent. As discussed by several authors, groups frequently engage in the social construction of knowledge, that is, they jointly produce knowledge, but that knowledge may then be used by an individual. In these instances, both the group and the individual learn, making it more difficult to distinguish which purposes are served by the learning—those of the individual or those of the group or, perhaps, both.

**Process Versus Content.** A theme closely related to the one discussed above is what I term an *essential tension* between the role of group process and the content or subject matter. According to Rose (Chapter One), the roots of this tension can be traced to Eduard Lindeman, and she suggests that "Lindeman's view of adult education as a process was his true major innovation." Thus from the formal founding of the field in the 1920s, the stage was set for what is sometimes an uneasy relationship between a group's process and the subject matter. This theme emerges in several other chapters (for example, Chapter Two by Imel and Tisdell, Chapter Five by Heimlich, and Chapter Four by Armstrong and Yarbrough), as the authors discuss the need to establish a balance between process and content for effective group learning to occur.

Again, a conundrum exists. Which is more important, the process of the group or the content that forms the basis for the learning? The answer seems to depend on the group's purpose and learning goals. In some groups, the emphasis may be on content, whereas in others the process may be more important. In discussing collaborative learning groups, for example, Cranton suggests that "process and content are inseparable here, unlike cooperative group learning where content is the primary focus." In the book groups described by Kerka (Chapter Nine), the process of discussion is an integral part of the learning activity. However, when the focus is on the group learning as an entity, as is described by West and by Drennon and Foucar-Szocki, the balance seems to shift toward an emphasis on process.

Using the learning continuum described earlier as a reference point, when the emphasis is on individual learning, content is stressed. As the purpose of learning moves along the continuum, away from individual learning toward the group learning as an entity, the relationship between process and content seems to be more balanced. When the purpose of learning moves to the end of the learning continuum that supports the group learning as an entity, process receives more emphasis. At all points on the continuum, however, both process and content have a role. The emphasis each receives, however, depends on the group's purpose and learning goals.

**Role of the Facilitator.** Again, closely related to the two previous themes is that of the role of the facilitator or group leader. Most authors mention facilitators or group leaders and discuss their roles. Most concur that the facilitator has some responsibility for establishing and maintaining the group learning environment and helping learners balance group maintenance and task functions, but varying perspectives emerge about how those roles should be performed. In her discussion of types of learning, Cranton says that facilitators' roles and responsibilities change to correspond to the group's purposes. Heimlich views the facilitator as the one who is responsible for constructing learning activities and managing their implementation. Drennon and Foucar-Szocki point out how a facilitator can model the philosophy or "stance" the group is expected to assume, in this case toward inquiry.

What may be more interesting and instructive for adult educators is what is said—or not said—about group facilitators in the chapters that focused on informal and workplace learning. In discussing how learning about technology occurs in work groups, Cahoon (Chapter Seven) describes a process in which leadership responsibility for the group seems to emerge and shift according to where the expertise lies. The learning emphasis in these work groups is definitely on content and helping a colleague learn that content. A process is in place that enables the groups to achieve their learning goals; an important part of this process is an understanding of where the expertise lies for solving a particular learning problem. In her discussion of book groups, Kerka points out that members prefer to share the responsibility for facilitation. In fact, for many adults, the appeal of book discussion groups lies in their un-school-like atmosphere, including the freedom to guide a group's own discussion.

The work group and book group examples demonstrate that adults are perfectly capable of learning in groups without the direction of a facilitator; however, a facilitator does have a role and purpose in many groups. Each learning group is unique, not only in terms of goals and purposes but also in terms of learner personalities, so requirements (and needs) for facilitation will change. Facilitation is best viewed as an art rather than a science. Because too many things related to the group are outside their control, adult educators should not fall into the trap of assuming "that for every facilitation problem, there is an appropriate technique that can be applied, if only one is experienced and competent enough" (Foley, 1992, pp. 158–159).

**Power Relations in Groups.** Throughout this volume, the theme of how power manifests itself in learning groups is much more subtle than the themes discussed previously. Only in Chapter Two is power a major topic. In that chapter, Tisdell and I highlight the need for more attention to power relations that are based on structural systems of privilege and oppression, such as gender, race, class, and sexual orientation. Because the theoretical foundations of the adult education literature on group relations tend to ignore these structural factors, little regard has been given to how they affect group dynamics. A few of the other chapters raise issues of power and the structural systems of privilege and oppression, but only indirectly. Rose and Kerka both describe how the emergence of women's groups in the nineteenth century came about because women were denied access to other educational opportunities, and Rose contrasts them with men's groups. Kerka also portrays differences in the type of discussion that goes on in women-only versus mixed groups, and she discusses the existence of unequal power relations between teachers and learners.

In discussing how individuals in work groups acquire information about technology, Cahoon refers to differences in status and authority among work group members. These factors have a bearing on how work groups negotiate informal rules for managing the distribution of computer knowledge and work. Although the power usually resides with those who have the greatest expertise, in one setting little group learning occurred because almost all the computer work was the responsibility of clerical staff "who lacked the political or cultural leverage to change the distribution of knowledge." In this case, the power that was related to structural factors such as class and position was more influential than power related to knowledge, a phenomena that has also been observed by Tisdell (1993) in a formal learning setting. In the electronic learning communities mentioned by Cahoon, structural factors were not in evidence, and power was ascribed to individuals solely on the basis of expertise. Cahoon's example confirms what has frequently been cited as an advantage of electronic learning communities, that is, they tend to level the playing field, because they cancel out structural factors such as race and class (but not gender).

Clearly, more attention needs to be given to power based on structural factors in learning groups. As adult educators, we need to become more aware of how it affects not only the dynamics of the group but also its impact on learning.

**Groups as Learning Communities.** The final theme selected for discussion—groups as learning communities—is only evident in Chapters Seven, Eight, and Nine. The learning groups described in these chapters include practitioner inquiry communities, electronic communities formed for the purpose of learning about technology, and book discussion groups. Although each chapter treats the theme of groups as learning communities a bit differently, each views the group as a place where members form relationships that extend beyond the learning task. The groups share some similar characteristics: they are informal in nature; they tend to operate without a formal facilitator, or in the case of the inquiry community, the facilitator has transferred ownership of the group to the members; and they are ongoing and not restricted by an artificially imposed schedule such as an academic calendar. Should a goal be to have every learning group become a learning community? As for many other aspects of learning groups, the answer depends on the goals and purposes of the group and the reasons for its formation. As conceived by Drennon and Foucar-Szocki, community is one of four interdependent dimensions of practitioner inquiry groups. For other types of groups, developing a sense of community may not be so necessary or important.

## Conclusion

Both the chapters and the areas selected for discussion here reflect some of the richness of group learning in adult education, and each could have been expanded. Clearly, the topic of groups in adult education needs more attention. More than one author pointed out the lack of research related to learning groups. Although research on groups and group process is plentiful in other disciplines, in recent years it has been a neglected area in adult education research. Also, adult educators need to turn their attention to how learning occurs in groups. The focus has been on helping groups work together, but now it needs to be on helping groups "become more aware of themselves as learning bodies" (Dechant, Marsick, and Kasl, 1993, p. 12). Part of this process should include thinking about how existing theories of adult learning apply in group learning situations. Additional study of informal learning groups could also shed light on how to change or improve learning groups in formal settings. And as discussed previously, the role of power in groups needs more attention.

Rather than remaining a subtext within the literature of the field, learning in groups needs to become a major theme. In the conclusion to Chapter One, Rose says that "while group learning lies at the heart of adult education, the process itself is almost taken for granted." It is time to shake off this taken-for-grantedness and give learning in groups the attention it deserves.

## References

Argyris, C., and Schön, D. M. *Theory in Practice: Improving Professional Effectiveness.* San Francisco: Jossey-Bass, 1977.

Dechant, K., Marsick, V. J., and Kasl, E. "Towards a Model of Team Learning." *Studies in Continuing Education,* 1993, 15 (1), 1–14.

Foley, G. "Going Deeper: Teaching and Group Work in Adult Education." *Studies in the Education of Adults,* 1992, 24 (2), 143–161.

Knights, B. "Hearing Yourself Teach: Group Processes for Adult Educators." *Studies in the Education of Adults,* 1993, 25 (2), 184–194.

Tisdell, E. "Interlocking Systems of Power, Privilege, and Oppression in Adult Higher Education Classes." *Adult Education Quarterly,* 1993, 43 (4), 203–226.

SUSAN IMEL *is senior research specialist at the Center on Education for Training and Employment, College of Education, The Ohio State University, where she serves as director of the ERIC Clearinghouse on Adult, Career, and Vocational Education.*

# INDEX

Abella, K. T., 44, 45
Activities, group, 42–43
Adler, M. J., 44
Administrators. *See* Practitioner inquiry groups
Adult education: adult basic education (ABE), 75–79; and book groups, 88–89; themes and issues, 91–95
Anderson, J. R., 65
Argyris, C., 53, 55, 56, 91
Arnold, C. C., 42
Asynchronous technology. *See* Technology, information
Autodidaxy, 3–5

Balcom, T., 82, 87
Barker, L. L., 41
Barriers to learning, 55–56
Bauman, P., 84, 85, 86, 87, 89
Beary, C., 42
Belzer, A., 71, 72
Benne, K. D., 9
Bennett, J. L., 63
Berger, P., 33
Berners-Lee, T., 62
Berry, M., 27
Beyer, B. K., 43
Bias against group activities, 15, 46
Biehler, R. F., 43, 47
Bikson, T. K., 61
Birkets, S., 89
Bloom, B. S., 42, 47
Book groups: adult learning in, 84–87; compared to school, 87–88, 93–94; history of, 81–82; nature of contemporary, 82–84
Bouwen, R., 52
Bradford, L. P., 9, 10
Brookfield, S., 44, 83, 85, 88
Brown, J. S., 61, 65
Brown, S., 4
Bullen, C. V., 63

Caffarella, R. S., 84
Cahoon, B., 61, 63
Candy, P. C., 89
Carlsen, M. B., 42

Case examples of group learning: with distributed computing, 65–68; power relations and conflict, 21–22; practitioner communities, 72–79; self-directed learning in collaborative groups, 30
Challenge, and group learning, 42–43
Cherfas, J., 45
Classroom issues, 71–72. *See also* Practitioner inquiry groups
Clemmer, J., 51, 55
Clubs, discussion: 19th century, 4–5, 12; 20th century, 5–7, 81–84
Collaborative (constructive) group learning, 18, 27–29, 31–32
Collins, A., 65
Color, people of, 21–22
Communicative knowledge, 25, 26, 27–29
Communities, Internet, 65–68
Communities, learning, 95; book groups, 81–89; electronic, 61–68; practitioner inquiry, 72–79. *See also* Members, group
Computer skills: group learning case studies, 66–68; learning, 63–65. *See also* Distributed computing; Technology, information
Conferencing, on-line, 63, 66–68
Conflict: and group learning, 42–43, 83; within groups, 19–22, 35
Consciousness-raising groups, women's, 11, 82
Construction of knowledge, social, 18, 27–29, 31–32
Content of instruction, 42–43; capturing, 57–58; focusing on, 46–47, 48; process versus, 92–93
Contexts of groups, types of, 36–37, 47–48
Cooperative (collected) group learning, 18, 26–27, 31, 42–43
Course, computer-based communication, 65
Cox, B., 65–66
Cragan, J. F., 17
Cranton, P., 31, 85, 89
Crook, C., 62

Cultural issues, within groups, 21–22
Culture: objectivity of, 29; of readers versus critics, 88

Debate or dialogue, group, 56–57, 83
Dechant, K., 16, 18, 19, 22, 33, 53, 54, 55, 95
Defensive routines, 55–57
deS. Brunner, E., 8, 9
Dialogue in learning, 56–57, 87–88
Discussion methods, 44; book group, 87–88
Distance education, 27
Distributed computing: group learning case study, 65–66; mailing lists, 62–63, 66–68; situated learning in, 63–65; terminology and background, 62–63
District of Columbia Public Library, 82
Diversity: among group members, 19, 21–22, 77, 83; of learning styles, 43
Documentation: of learning in groups, 46–47, 48, 57–58; practitioner inquiry, 76–77
Double-loop learning, 52–53, 56
Draves, W. A., 46
Drennon, C., 79
Duguid, P., 61, 65
Dworkin, M. S., 41

Educator roles, and types of group learning, 27, 29, 30–31. *See also* Facilitator roles
Eggen, P., 44
Electronic communication. *See* Technology, information
Ely, M. L., 7
E-mail, 62
Emancipatory learning, 25, 26; group, 29–31
Empowerment of learners, 29–31, 32, 52–53, 54–55
Environments, group, 33–34, 38–39, 95; book group, 82–84; context variables, 36–37, 47–48; informal, 63–64, 66–68, 94; internal, 34–36, 85; perceptions of, 37–38, 92; practitioner inquiry community, 71–72
Etiquette. *See* Power relations, group; Rules, group

Facilitator roles, 84, 93–94; in collaborative group learning, 29, 31; constructing activities, 42–43; in cooperative group learning, 27; of educators, 27, 29, 30–31; in forming learning subgroups, 19; and group process, 18–19, 31, 42–43; and techniques, 44–46; tips for, 46–48; in transformative group learning, 30–31. *See also* Leadership, group
Farquharson, A., 27
Fellenz, R. A., 44, 45
Flood, J., 82, 85, 86
Foley, G., 17, 18, 20, 21, 22–23, 94
Folinsbee, S. W., 53
Follett, M. P., 5
Four C's, the (conflict, cooperation, challenge, content), 42–43
Freire, P., 10–11
Frontier-Talk mailing list, 66–68
Fry, R., 52

Galagan, P. A., 52
Gaming, group, 45
Gardner, H., 43
Garvin, D. A., 57, 58
Gender and group discussion, 84
General Education Development (GED) class, 74
George Mason University, 65–66
Georgia Adult Literacy Practitioner Inquiry Network (GALPIN), 72–74
Gibb, J. R., 9
Gilstrap, R. L., 44
Gist, M. E., 63
GNN (Global Navigator Network) Story Café, 82
Great Books movement, 82, 83
Ground rules, group, 47, 94
Group adult education: and book groups, 84–87; historical roots of, 3–12, 81–82; in learning organizations, 54–58
Group development: in learning organizations, 54–58, 65–66; into practitioner inquiry groups, 74–79; process, 17–18, 35–36; and rules, 47, 67, 87, 94; size and membership issues, 19, 84; stages of, 17–18, 35–36; tips for, 46–48
Group Environment Scale (GES), 38
Group learning: collaborative, 18, 27–29, 31–32; common methods for, 44–46; constructing activities for, 42–43; cooperative, 18, 26–27, 31; and distributed computing, 65–68; environments, 34–38; historical roots of, 3–12, 81–82; and intention, 75–76, 92–93; models,

18, 34–38; the nature of adult, 15–23, 55–56, 63–65, 91–95; negative factors, 15, 46; and order, 76–77; overlooked tenets of, 34; perceptions of, 37–38, 87–88, 92; themes and issues, 91–95; types of, 25–32, 92, 95

Group process theory, 41–42; versus content, 92–93; on facilitator roles, 18–19, 31, 42–43; and leadership issues, 21–22, 84, 93–94; on maintenance and task functions, 17; power and conflict issues, 19–21, 42; and skills, 85–86. *See also* Group development

Group theory: diversity of, 16; history of, 7–8; legitimate peripheral participation, 64–65; related to learning groups, 15–16, 33–34

Gulley, H. D., 41

Habermas, J., 1, 25, 27
Hart, M. U., 11
Hayes, E., 28, 29
Heimlich, J. E., 47, 83, 84, 85
Highet, G., 46
History, of distributed computing, 62–63
History of group adult education, 11–12; autodidaxy and club learning, 3–5; in book groups, 81–82; and group discussion, 5–7, 81–82; and 1940s–1950s group theory, 7–8; from 1960s on, 8–11, 82–84; in organizations, 52–54; self-help groups, 11; for social change, 10–11; T-groups (training-groups), 9–10
Hoffer, J. A., 17
Hollingshead, A. B., 62
Horton, M., 10
Hospital group environment, 38
Houle, C. O., 8
Hughes, H., 82–83, 84, 87
Human interests, kinds of, 25–26
Hutchins, E. L., 63, 68

Imel, S., 18, 25, 27, 33
Individual learning: autodidaxy, 3–5; shift to group learning, 18
Informal group learning, 63–64, 94. *See also* Environments, group
Information, group. *See* Documentation; Technology, information
Inquiry groups. *See* Practitioner inquiry groups
Instrumental knowledge, 25, 26–27

Intergroup effect, 19
Internal environment, group, 34–36, 85
Internet communication: book discussion groups, 82; learning communities, 66–68; terminology, 62–63
Isaacs, W. N., 55, 56, 57

Jacobs, R. L., 59
Jacobsen, D., 44
Jacobsohn, R. W., 82, 83, 84, 85, 86
Jaques, D., 17, 19
Jaquette, V., 82
Jarvis, P., 18, 29, 42
Jick, T., 58
Jones, K., 45
Journal writing, 46
Joyce, B., 41
Juechter, W. M., 52
Just-in-time learning, 65, 68

Kagan, S., 27
Kahn, T. M., 52
Kasl, E., 16, 18, 19, 22, 33, 53, 54, 55, 95
Kasulis, T. P., 44
Kauchak, D., 44
Keane, P., 10
Kerka, S., 59
Kett, J., 3
Kim, D. H., 57, 58
Kirchner, C., 8, 9
Knights, B., 1, 15, 18, 19, 20, 22, 91
Knowledge: book group types of, 85–87; computer skill, 63–65, 67–68; day-to-day practice, 72; deferred or just-in-time, 65, 68; kinds of human interests and, 25–26, 86; of self and others, 86, 88; social construction of, 27–29, 33, 92; and voice, 78–79
Knowles, H., 7–8
Knowles, M., 7–8
Kofman, F., 33–34, 55
Konopka, G., 5, 6

Landauer, T. K., 62
Laskin, D., 82–83, 84, 87
Lave, J., 63, 64
Lawson, D. E., 41
Leadership, group, 84, 93–94; and class and cultural issues, 21–22. *See also* Facilitator roles
Learning: barriers to, 55–56; capturing, 57–58; computer skill, 63–65; continuum of individual and group, 92, 93;

organizational, 52–53; perceptions of, 87–88, 92; respecting differing styles of, 43. *See also* Group learning
Learning organizations, 53, 54–58
Legitimate peripheral participation, 64–65
Lessons from group activity, 48
Levine, J. M., 16, 19, 20
Lewin, K., 7, 9, 11
Lieberman, M. A., 5–6, 11
Lindeman, E. C., 5–6, 11, 92
Lippitt, R. O., 9
Literacy teachers inquiry group, 72–74
Literature, types of knowledge from, 85–87
Local area networks. *See* Distributed computing
Local experts, learning from, 64, 67, 93
Long, E., 86, 88
Lovell, R. B., 41
Luke, R. A., 10
Lytle, S. L., 71, 72

Macfarlane, E. C., 82
MacGregor, J., 27, 29
McCaulley, M. H., 43
McGrath, J. E., 62
Mailing lists, electronic, 62–63, 66–68
Main, C., 27
Maintenance functions, group, 17, 84
Marshall, J. D., 83, 85, 86, 87, 88
Marsick, V. J., 16, 18, 19, 22, 33, 51, 53, 54, 55, 58, 95
Martin, T. P., 4
Martin, W. R., 44
Mechanized method of learning, 52
Members, group: behavior progression in, 35–36; book group, 82–87; defensive routines among, 55–57; dialogue among, 56–57, 84; diversity of, 19, 77, 83–84; inquiry community, 74–79; interdependence of, 34–35, 75–76; people of color as, 21–22; safety for self-disclosure by, 47–48, 56–57, 78, 83, 84; social environment of, 36–37, 47–48, 55–56, 77–78. *See also* Communities, learning
Memory and learning, 57–58
Mennecke, B. E., 17
Men's clubs, 4
Merriam, S. B., 84
Mezirow, J., 18, 25, 27, 29, 30, 55, 57
Miller, J. E., 18, 19
Miller, N., 9
Moore, T., 83

Moos, R. H., 38
Morale, group, 38
Moreland, R. L., 16, 19, 20
Myers, I. B., 43

National Center on Adult Literacy (NCAL), 71
Neidorf, R. M., 82, 83, 84
Networks: electronic, 58, 62–63; learning, 85; practitioner inquiry group, 72–74. *See also* Book groups
Newberry, J. S., 8, 9
Nilson, C., 44
Norland, E., 47
Novak, J. D., 45

O'Connor, T. F., 81
Oleson, A., 4
Oliver, L. P., 28
Olsten Forum for Information Management, 61
On-the-job training and learning, 53, 63–65; via distributed computing, 66–68
Organizations: group learning in, 33–34, 63–65; group members' perceptions of, 37–38, 87–88

Paideia Program, 44
Palazzolo, C., 33
Palmer, H., 43
Palmore, S. N., 82
Participation in groups, encouraging, 46–47, 87–88
Participatory learning. *See* Transformative group learning
Pearlman, M., 82, 83, 84
Peers, learning from, 64, 66–68
Pelletier, C. M., 82
Perceptions, environment and group, 37–38, 87–88, 92
Poststructural theory, 20–21
Powell, J. W., 8
Power relations, group, 64, 84, 94–95; in book groups, 87–88; and conflict issues, 19–21, 35, 42–43, 83; personal and position, 31; and rules, 47, 67, 87, 94; and structural systems of privilege, 19–21, 94; teacher and student, 66
Practitioner inquiry groups, 71, 80; challenges to, 79; GALPIN example of, 72–74; group development into, 74–79; intention, 75–76
Productivity paradox, 63

Projects, group, 45–46, 73–74
Psychology: humanistic, 20–21; social, 33

Reading: enthusiasm for, 73–74, 89; types of knowledge from, 85–87. *See also* Book groups
Research, practitioner inquiry: dimensions of, 74–79; projects, 73–74
Research needed: on group process theory and learning theory, 22–23; on learning groups and adult education, 95; on structural factors and power in groups, 94–95
Retention, adult learner, 74
Reumann, R., 71, 72
Robson, M., 42
Role play, group, 45, 86
Rosen, B., 63
Rubin, J. S., 5
Rules, group, 47, 67, 87, 94

Saal, R., 84
Safety and self-disclosure within groups, 47–48, 56–57, 78, 83, 84
Santayana, G., 57
Saving face, 56
Schein, E. H., 55, 56, 57
Schied, F. M., 59
Schön, D., 18, 91
School, reading groups compared to, 87–88
Schwoerer, C., 63
Seaman, D. F., 44, 45
Self-education, 3–5, 86, 88
Self-help groups, 11
Sells, S., 36–37
Senge, P., 33–34, 53, 54, 55, 56, 57, 58
Shaftel, F. R., 45
Shaftel, G., 45
Sibbet, D., 52–53
Simic, M. R., 82
Simpson, G. W., 27
Simulations, group, 45
Singley, M. K., 65
Situated learning, 63–65
Size of learning groups, 19, 84
Slavin, R., 26
Slezak, E., 82, 83, 84, 86, 87
Smagorinsky, P., 83, 85, 86, 87, 88
Smith, S. W., 83, 85, 86, 87, 88
Snowman, J., 43, 47
Social change, education for, 10–11, 31
Social environments of groups, 36–39

Staff development. *See* Practitioner inquiry groups
Stengel, C., 51
Stewart, D., 6
Structural systems, and group process, 19–21, 94
Stubblefield, H. W., 10
Studebaker, J. W., 6–7
Sutton-Smith, B., 45
Swanson, A., 85–86, 87, 88
Synchronous technologies, 62
Systems model of team learning, 54

Taming the Electronic Frontier (course), 65–66
Task functions, group, 17
Teachers. *See* Facilitator roles; Practitioner inquiry groups
Technical education, 27
Technology, information: access to, 21; and group learning, 61–68, 89
T-groups (training-groups), 9–10
Thelen, H. A., 41
Theories-in-use, 55, 91. *See also* Group theory
Therapy groups, 11
Think-feel-believe rule, 47
Tisdell, E. J., 21–22, 94
Training, teacher, 75–79
Training classrooms, 53
Transformative group learning, 29–31, 32, 54–55
Trimbur, J., 18, 19
Tuckman, B. W., 17
Tutoring by local experts, 64, 67–68, 93

Ulrich, D., 58
User groups, computer, 62–63, 65–68

Vella, J., 45
Visualization techniques, 46, 74
Voice: and gender in groups, 84; of inquiry communities, 78–79; and structural privilege, 21–22
Von Glinow, M. A., 58
Voss, J., 4

Wagner, R. H., 42
Walter, P. G., 28, 29
Watkins, K. E., 51, 53, 58
Web, the. *See* World Wide Web
Weil, M., 41
Wenger, E., 63, 64
West, G. W., 59

White privilege issues, 21–22
Wilder, D. S., 8, 9
Wilkes, J. M., 18, 19
Willens, S. P., 89
Williams, L. V., 43
Winer, D., 67
Women's groups: and book groups, 81–82, 83–84; consciousness-raising, 11, 82; 19th century clubs, 4–5, 12, 81, 94
Wooley, D. R., 63
Woolfolk, A. E., 43, 47
Work group learning, 63–65, 93–94

Workplace: changing paradigms in, 52; group learning, 53–54, 66–68; the Internet, 66–68; types of learning in, 52–53
World Wide Web, the, 62, 66–68, 82. *See also* Internet communication
Wright, D. W., 17
Wynne, B. E., 17

Yalom, I. D., 48
Yarbrough, S., 38

Zander, A., 19

# Ordering Information

NEW DIRECTIONS FOR ADULT AND CONTINUING EDUCATION is a series of paperback books that explores issues of common interest to instructors, administrators, counselors, and policy makers in a broad range of adult and continuing education settings—such as colleges and universities, extension programs, businesses, the military, prisons, libraries, and museums. Books in the series are published quarterly in Spring, Summer, Fall, and Winter and are available for purchase by subscription and individually.

SUBSCRIPTIONS cost $52.00 for individuals (a savings of 35 percent over single-copy prices) and $79.00 for institutions, agencies, and libraries. Standing orders are accepted. New York residents, add local sales tax for subscriptions. (For subscriptions outside the United States, add $7.00 for shipping via surface mail or $25.00 for air mail. Orders *must be prepaid* in U.S. dollars by check drawn on a U.S. bank or charged to VISA, MasterCard, or American Express.)

SINGLE COPIES cost $20.00 plus shipping (see below) when payment accompanies order. California, New Jersey, New York, and Washington, D.C., residents, please include appropriate sales tax. Canadian residents, add GST and any local taxes. Billed orders will be charged shipping and handling. No billed shipments to post office boxes. (Orders from outside the United States *must be prepaid* in U.S. dollars by check drawn on a U.S. bank or charged to VISA, MasterCard, or American Express.)

SHIPPING (SINGLE COPIES ONLY): one issue, add $5.00; two issues, add $6.00; three issues, add $7.00; four to five issues, add $8.00; six to seven issues, add $9.00; eight or more issues, add $12.00.

ALL PRICES are subject to change.

DISCOUNTS FOR QUANTITY ORDERS are available. Please write to the address below for information.

ALL ORDERS must include either the name of an individual or an official purchase order number. Please submit your order as follows:
 *Subscriptions:* specify series and year subscription is to begin
 *Single copies:* include individual title code (such as ACE 59)

MAIL ALL ORDERS TO:
 Jossey-Bass Publishers
 350 Sansome Street
 San Francisco, California 94104-1342

FOR SUBSCRIPTION SALES OUTSIDE OF THE UNITED STATES, contact any international subscription agency or Jossey-Bass directly.

OTHER TITLES AVAILABLE IN THE
NEW DIRECTIONS FOR ADULT AND CONTINUING EDUCATION SERIES
*Ralph G. Brockett, Susan Imel,* Editors-in-Chief
*Alan B. Knox,* Consulting Editor

| | |
|---|---|
| ACE70 | A Community-Based Approach to Literacy Programs: Taking Learners' Lives into Account, *Peggy A. Sissel* |
| ACE69 | What Really Matters in Adult Education Program Planning: Lessons in Negotiating Power and Interests, *Ronald M. Cervero, Arthur L. Wilson* |
| ACE68 | Workplace Learning, *W. Franklin Spikes* |
| ACE67 | Facilitating Distance Education, *Mark H. Rossman, Maxine E. Rossman* |
| ACE66 | Mentoring: New Strategies and Challenges, *Michael W. Galbraith, Norman H. Cohen* |
| ACE65 | Learning Environments for Women's Adult Development: Bridges Toward Change, *Kathleen Taylor, Catherine Marienau* |
| ACE64 | Overcoming Resistance to Self-Direction in Adult Learning, *Roger Hiemstra, Ralph G. Brockett* |
| ACE63 | The Emerging Power of Action Inquiry Technologies, *Ann Brooks, Karen E. Watkins* |
| ACE62 | Experiential Learning: A New Appproach, *Lewis Jackson, Rosemary S. Caffarella* |
| ACE61 | Confronting Racism and Sexism, *Elisabeth Hayes, Scipio A. J. Colin III* |
| ACE60 | Current Perspectives on Administration of Adult Education Programs, *Patricia Mulcrone* |
| ACE59 | Applying Cognitive Learning Theory to Adult Learning, *Daniele D. Flannery* |
| ACE58 | The Adult Educator as Consultant, *Lois J. Zachary, Sally Vernon* |
| ACE57 | An Update on Adult Learning Theory, *Sharan B. Merriam* |
| ACE56 | Rethinking Leadership in Adult and Continuing Education, *Paul J. Edelson* |
| ACE55 | Professionals' Ways of Knowing: New Findings on How to Improve Professional Education, *H. K. Morris Baskett, Victoria J. Marsick* |
| ACE54 | Confronting Controversies in Challenging Times: A Call for Action, *Michael W. Galbraith, Burton R. Sisco* |
| ACE53 | Learning for Personal Development, *Lorraine A. Cavaliere, Angela Sgroi* |
| ACE52 | Perspectives on Educational Certificate Programs, *Margaret E. Holt, George J. Lopos* |
| ACE51 | Professional Development for Educators of Adults, *Ralph G. Brockett* |
| ACE50 | Creating Environments for Effective Adult Learning, *Roger Hiemstra* |
| ACE49 | Mistakes Made and Lessons Learned: Overcoming Obstacles to Successful Program Planning, *Thomas J. Sork* |
| ACE48 | Serving Culturally Diverse Populations, *Jovita M. Ross-Gordon, Larry G. Martin, Diane Buck Briscoe* |
| ACE47 | Education Through Community Organizations, *Michael W. Galbraith* |
| ACE45 | Applying Adult Development Strategies, *Mark H. Rossman, Maxine E. Rossman* |
| CE44 | Fulfilling the Promise of Adult and Continuing Education, *B. Allan Quigley* |
| CE43 | Effective Teaching Styles, *Elisabeth Hayes* |
| CE42 | Participatory Literacy Education, *Arlene Fingeret, Paul Jurmo* |
| CE41 | Recruiting and Retaining Adult Students, *Peter S. Cookson* |
| CE32 | Issues in Adult Career Counseling, *Juliet V. Miller, Mary Lynne Musgrove* |
| CE31 | Marketing Continuing Education, *Hal Beder* |
| CE25 | Self-Directed Learning: From Theory to Practice, *Stephen Brookfield* |
| CE22 | Designing and Implementing Effective Workshops, *Thomas J. Sork* |
| CE19 | Helping Adults Learn How to Learn, *Robert M. Smith* |

# Statement of Ownership, Management, and Circulation

*(Required by 39 U.S.C. 3685)*

**1. Publication Title:** NEW DIRECTIONS FOR ADULT AND CONTINUING EDUCATION
**2. Publication No.:** 1052-2891
**3. Filing Date:** 9/26/96
**4. Issue Frequency:** QUARTERLY
**5. No. of Issues Published Annually:** 4
**6. Annual Subscription Price:** $52 – indiv. / $79 – instit.
**7. Complete Mailing Address of Known Office of Publication:** 350 SANSOME STREET, SAN FRANCISCO, CA 94104 (SAN FRANCISCO COUNTY)
**8. Complete Mailing Address of Headquarters or General Business Office of Publisher:** SAME AS ABOVE
**9. Full Names and Complete Mailing Addresses of Publisher, Editor, and Managing Editor:**
- Publisher: JOSSEY-BASS INC., PUBLISHERS (SAME AS ABOVE)
- Editor: SUSAN IMEL, CENTER FOR TRAINING AND EMPLOYMENT, THE OHIO STATE UNIVERSITY, 1900 KENNY ROAD, COLUMBUS, OH 43210-1090
- Managing Editor: NONE

**10. Owner:**

| Full Name | Complete Mailing Address |
|---|---|
| SIMON & SCHUSTER, INC. | P.O. BOX 1172, ENGLEWOOD CLIFFS, NJ 07632-1172 |

**11. Known Bondholders, Mortgagees, and Other Security Holders Owning or Holding 1 Percent or More of Total Amount of Bonds, Mortgages, or Other Securities:**

| Full Name | Complete Mailing Address |
|---|---|
| SAME AS ABOVE | SAME AS ABOVE |

**12. For completion by nonprofit organizations:** Has Not Changed During Preceding 12 Months

**13. Publication Name:** NEW DIRECTIONS FOR ADULT AND CONTINUING EDUCATION
**14. Issue Date for Circulation Data Below:** SPRING 1996

**15. Extent and Nature of Circulation**

| | Average No. Copies Each Issue During Preceding 12 Months | Actual No. Copies of Single Issue Published Nearest to Filing Date |
|---|---|---|
| a. Total No. Copies (Net Press Run) | 1548 | 1574 |
| b. Paid and/or Requested Circulation (1) Sales Through Dealers and Carriers, Street Vendors, and Counter Sales (Not Mailed) | 202 | 117 |
| (2) Paid or Requested Mail Subscriptions (Include Advertisers' Proof Copies/Exchange Copies) | 794 | 866 |
| c. Total Paid and/or Requested Circulation (Sum of 15b(1) and 15b(2)) | 996 | 983 |
| d. Free Distribution by Mail (Samples, Complimentary, and Other Free) | 74 | 75 |
| e. Free Distribution Outside the Mail (Carriers or Other Means) | 0 | 0 |
| f. Total Free Distribution (Sum of 15d and 15e) | 74 | 75 |
| g. Total Distribution (Sum of 15c and 15f) | 1070 | 1058 |
| h. Copies Not Distributed (1) Office Use, Leftovers, Spoiled | 478 | 516 |
| (2) Return from News Agents | 0 | 0 |
| i. Total (Sum of 15g, 15h(1), and 15h(2)) | 1548 | 1574 |
| Percent Paid and/or Requested Circulation (15c / 15g x 100) | 93% | 93% |

**16.** This Statement of Ownership will be printed in the WINTER 1996 issue of this publication.

**17. Signature and Title of Editor, Publisher, Business Manager, or Owner:** SUSAN E. LEWIS, PERIODICALS DIRECTOR
**Date:** 9/26/96